Stories and Principles

About

Raising Children

Ruth Towns

with Elmer L. Towns

Stories and Principles About Raising Children
by Ruth Towns with Elmer L. Towns

ISBN 13 Trade Paper: 978-0-7684-5941-8
ISBN 13 eBook: 978-0-7684-5942-5

DEDICATION

TO THE GREATEST MOM AND WIFE—

RUTH TOWNS
1932 - 2013

Ruth was always there for our children while I was at school, or out preaching or away on a trip. Ruth felt it was her calling from God to be home with the kids. Ruth gets all the credit for our kids.

I stepped in to teach during these experiences described in this book. Ruth was the all-day teacher and the all-experience teacher and the all-times teacher. She was the great teacher.

Lack of money was always a problem. While I was out trying to get it, I wasn't always faced with a lack of it. Ruth had to stay at home and make do with little money and give our children what they needed, less than we could afford. In spite of constant financial pressures, she got us through.

I wasn't always patient with the children. Ruth was always kind, always patient with the children and long-suffering with me. I tell my Sunday school class, "I married a gentle woman."

This book should be about her and the children, not what I did. But since I'm the "storyteller" in the family, I wrote what I remember about them.

Because she is the best, the kids and I dedicate this book to her.

TABLE OF CONTENTS

Chapter

Introduction: THE SWING SET: Don't Make Them Live Out Your Dreams. 11

To teach character, a parent must begin where their children are, and lead them to where they should be.

1   AIR SNAKES: Don't Be Gullible. 15

I told my children a unique kind of fairy tale to help them recognize truth.

2   MAKING BOOKS: Can We Go to McDonald's? 25

The kids helped me assemble books that I sold, so we could all go to McDonald's.

3   THE CUBS: Ya Gotta Root for Someone. 33

I helped my son build loyalty to a baseball team.

4   THE CAMERA AND BALL GLOVE: Learning Honesty. 45

My wife showed the kids how to return lost articles to the owner yet keep them with integrity.

5   CLASSIC COMICS: Learning Responsibility. 53

The kids read over 100 comic books of the outstanding
Literary Masterpieces.

6   MONOPOLY: When Losing is Winning. 61

I taught the kids to play Monopoly to develop their
instinct for winning. But I did it too well.

7   THE PHOTO CONTEST: Teaching Creativity. 69

Because I wanted them to remember what they saw on
a cross-country auto trip, I planned a photo contest.

8   AWANA: Make Me Learn. 79

It was important for Sam to learn the things I learned
in Boy Scouts.

9   HORSESHOES: You Can Do It. 85

Sam was more comfortable around world-class scholars
than I was.

10   WORKING IN MEXICO: A New Horizon of Growth. 91

Debbie learned to serve the Lord, "two-piling cement"
in Mexico.

11   PRAYING FOR A MUSEUM: Sharing Spiritual Lessons...101

My son challenged me to pray for something I always
wanted but had never asked God to give to me.

12 PICKING UP FIREWOOD: Doing More Than Expected. ...113

Usually kids do less than you request, but this time they did more than expected.

13 "B-U-T-T": You Can't Say That. 123

I wouldn't let the girls use crude language. I wanted them to be refined.

14 REMLE NOEL: Singing Who You Are. 129

Why is it that every generation disliked the music of its kids? Is it because what we sing defines who we are?

15 THE MISSIONARY CLOSET: Back Door to the Best........137

God provided Neiman Marcus clothes when we couldn't afford a K-Mart "Bluelight Special."

16 MOVIES: Not Going No Longer. 143

Originally, we wouldn't let the kids attend movies; changing our policy was an educational process.

17 I SPY: Developing the Power of Observation. 151

We played games around the table to develop their power of observation.

18 CHRISTMAS TREE ORNAMENTS: Building Future Expectations 157

We did it the same way every year at Christmas, creating in the kids a confident expectation of the future.

19 FIRST CARS: Taking Responsibility. 165

We came up with a unique formula that allowed each child to purchase their first car with our help.

APPENDIX

A. THE TOWNS' WAY: HOW TO TEACH CHARACTER TO CHILDREN 173

It takes more than one day and one lesson to build character in your children. The Towns' Way is a cycle that is a total approach to forming their character.

INTRODUCTION

THE SWING SET: DON'T MAKE THEM LIVE OUT YOUR DREAMS

Growing up, I always wanted a swing set. I had seen in the *Children Activities* magazine a dream of a tall set of red pipes that held aloft a swing on chains, a blue sliding board and a yellow teeter-totter. It's called a swing set by modern families, but in the old days it was also called a jungle gym. There was a swing set at the city playground, where I played on the way home from school. It was built of drab galvanized steel pipes. Playing on the swing set in the city park didn't satisfy me; it only enhanced my desire to own one. I always dreamed of having my own private red jungle gym right in my own backyard. I could close my eyes and see the blue sliding board and bright yellow see-saw. But I never got it.

After I was married, I bought a gleaming red swing set for my kids. I scraped together all the extra money I could find and bought a Sears and Roebuck jungle gym. It cost $9.99 in the 1950s.

The backyard was dark when I got home. So, with a flashlight and open blinds in the dining room for a little extra light, I assembled the red pipes, chains and sliding board before going to bed. I expected my kids to rush out before breakfast to play on it all morning. I expected they would beg to stay out and play. I expected them to fuss when we called them in for breakfast. I expected Debbie to plead,

"Let us play...we're not hungry..."

After breakfast, they ran out to swing, slide and bump on the see-saw. When Ruth called them for breakfast, they obediently came without a whimper. They didn't have my passion for the red jungle gym. It didn't captivate them as I had been addicted to its picture in the children's magazine.

"IF I HAD ONE," I thought, "I'D NEVER COME IN THE HOUSE."

My kids politely swayed in the swings but there was no compulsive love affair with the red swing set. Two days later Debbie came home with muddied feet, a bruised elbow and buttons torn off her play suit.

"You should see our rope," she proclaimed to Ruth. "We swing a mile," she exaggerated.

Debbie babbled about the newfound love of her life. Outside our subdivision she found a rope swing in an old apple tree that gracefully covered the intersection of two ditches. The kids could swing from one high dirt bank to the other. Someone had hung a rope from an enticing limb and tied a sack full of hay to the dangling end. Not only was it a long swing, but each time Debbie swung close to the bank, someone leaped out into the ditch and caught the rope to "hitch" a ride. As a kid I called it "hoboing."

Debbie's swing in the apple tree taught me it doesn't take money to make your kids happy. And a second principle I learned, your kids don't always have fun doing the things you dreamed of doing, so don't try to live your dreams through them.

This jungle gym story is similar to the stories you'll find in each chapter. Those stories reflect the struggles Ruth and I had learning how to raise our children. I hope you can identify your struggles with our attempts. And just as I suggested two lessons I learned from the swing in the apple tree, each chapter will attempt to spell out the principles my wife and I learned as we overcame the obstacles that filled the path of child rearing.

Producing character in your children is the greatest challenge to modern parents. I define character as, "Habitually doing the right thing in the right way." This book tells how my wife and I tried to transfer our positive values into our three children, Debbie, Sam and Polly.

This book is not a textbook of principles for you to teach your children, although at the end of each chapter, I include principles that grew out of our raising our kids.

The stories are intended to make you smile because some are funny. Other stories will create anxiety because when you read what I did wrong, you also realize you made the same mistakes. Whatever the story, I want you to feel our experiences. My prayer is that each chapter will lead into biblical principles and we will all do it better.

My wife and children have read the manuscript and have been given editorial authority to take out anything that wasn't accurate or add anything to make it right.

I wrote this book around 1998 when the kids were all around 40 years old.

As I publish this manuscript (2020), Debbie has retired from being a supervisor in the computerized mail sort section of the U.S. Post Office. She has two married daughters and three grandchildren. Sam was Assistant Dean of Religion of the External Degree Program at Liberty University, Lynchburg, Virginia. He was killed in an auto accident on January 26, 2002. He had two children. Polly is a successful realtor in Lynchburg, Virginia and has two married daughters.

Ruth and I have ten grandchildren by birth and marriage. Also, we have six great-grandchildren. Ruth was the director of an adoption agency, Family Life Service, Lynchburg, Virginia. I was Dean of the School of Religion and Liberty Baptist Seminary at Liberty University and Vice President.

May God use this manuscript for the purpose for which it was written, to help people do a better job of rearing their children. My prayer is that God would use that which is usable and blot out of people's memory that which is harmful.

Sincerely yours in Christ,

Elmer Towns

From my home on Liberty Mountain

March 2020

CHAPTER ONE

AIR SNAKES: DON'T BE GULLIBLE

"Race you to the top" Debbie yelled to Polly as we were climbing Kennesaw Mountain in North Georgia. It was 1961 and we were really not mountain climbing in the classical definition. We didn't have ropes to pull one another up a rock cliff. Kennesaw was a State Park and our family was walking up a paved sidewalk to the top.

"You can't beat me," seven-year-old Debbie challenged her younger sister Polly who was only three at the time. But I was afraid that when they got to the top, they would play too close to the edge of the cliff. It was dangerous to be up there without adults.

Ruth and I were walking slower. I tried to think of some way to keep them from the dangerous edge of the cliff. Then suddenly without thinking it through I yelled,

"Watch out for the air snakes..."

Debbie stopped running... she turned around to challenge me,

"Snakes can't fly..." I said the first thing that came to my mind so I had yelled, "Watch out for air snakes." Now I had to give some credibility to my warning. "WHAT WOULD THEY BELIEVE," I pondered.

"See those tall bushes on the side of the path" I pointed to the heavy foliage taller than either Debbie or Polly. The bushes had heavy dark green leaves. Tall weeds growing up through the bushes ... a wet murky place where snakes might hide.

"Air snakes hide in these tall bushes..." I was searching for credibility. "They don't really fly..." I made up the story on the spot. "Air snakes spring at you from the bushes like a coiled snake on the ground..."

Debbie and Polly didn't know whether to believe me or not. After all there could be snakes in the bushes ready to spring out at them. So I padded the story.

"Air snakes have gills that make them look like they are flying" I explained. "When they spring out at you, they kinda glide toward you..."

Both girls stopped dead still. Then began to examine the tops of the bushes above their hands.

"Get in the middle of the path" I explained. "That way they won't drop on you."

Both girls jumped to the middle of the path. My air snake story was manufactured on the spot, but it achieved its intent. The girls stayed on the path and away from the dangerous cliff. We walked to the visitors overlook and enjoyed the scene from which a battle between Northern and Southern troops was fought during the Civil War. Then we turned and walked back down the path. One of the girls asked.

"Can air snakes hurt you?"

"Don't worry about them," I explained. "No one has ever died from air snakes." That was a true statement. No one could be harmed by a snake that wasn't real. Then I added,

"They are slow and clumsy. If they land on you, it takes several minutes for them to pull back their heads to strike." I added, "the air is thin up here."

If I had made believers of the kids on the way up, I destroyed my credibility with the part about their being slow. Now they didn't believe me.

"That's not true..." Sam concluded.

In the car we laughed about air snakes. We did more than talk; we made up more stories about air snakes. We exaggerated the actions of air snakes and imitated air snakes falling out of bushes and imitated their bite on the back of our hands.

There are defining moments in life, and the "air snake" story is one that stayed with my children. I made up a story to answer a child's question. The story was fiction, but believable ... it was harmless but instructional ... it was far-fetched but something about the story made it hard to deny. It had credibility.

From that experience on, the whole Towns family called the stories I made up "Air Snakes."

Don't think of me as cruel or misleading my children. I wasn't lying to them in the way Webster's Dictionary defines lying. I was telling them the Fairy Tales or Nursery Rhymes of Elmer Towns.

No one tells children about GoldiLocks and the three bears to lie to them. A fairy tale is part teaching morals, part entertaining and sometimes we use nursery rhymes like "Jack and the Bean Stalk" (an obvious exaggeration) for devious purposes. Parents pretend to entertain, when they deviously try to put the little fellow to sleep.

Someone accused me of scaring my children with stories of snakes that are exaggerated to fly. What about the tales of Mother Goose? What about three pigs boiling a wolf in water, or another wolf that eats Little Red Riding Hood's Grandmother... isn't that squeamish?

The Towns children didn't get nursery rhymes, they got Air Snakes. Air Snake stories were cute. I didn't want to tell them about the good tooth fairy, the fable most parents tell their children when a baby tooth drops out. That's the unlikely story of a fairy sneaking in the child's room at night while they are sleeping to take away their tooth and leave some money.

When Debbie lost her first molar, I forgot to take the tooth and leave money. The next morning, she was so disappointed, that I made up another air snake story I told her that molars are too heavy for fairies and that the tooth gorilla would have to retrieve her tooth.

Debbie has even shared this story with her children and grandchildren.

"The Good Tooth Gorilla will bring you a quarter" I told Debbie, "But you've got to put the tooth under your pillow when you go to sleep."

It never occurred to me that the idea of a huge hairy gorilla tip-toeing into her room might frighten or give her nightmares.

"The Good Tooth Gorilla doesn't make any noise" I tried to motivate her to go to sleep. "If you stay awake to see the Good Tooth Gorilla, he won't leave you anything," I continued, "so go to sleep."

I'm not sure Ruth went along with my Tooth Gorilla idea. She probably told them about a Tinker Bell-type Tooth Fairy after I left the room.

A good Air Snake had to be believable, and the more credibility the story when I told it, the better. One of my famous Air Snakes was the "Tongue of the Tide."

The family was fishing for crabs in a flat-bottom rowboat in Bonna Bella, near my birth home in Savannah, Georgia. I always rented a boat on a small river, i.e. the Herb River so my kids could enjoy the experiences I had as a child. I wanted my kids to experience crabbing like I had as a child. Then rowing about a half mile, I headed the nose of the boat into a narrow creek, just wide enough for the boat, not wide enough to put my oars into the water. So, I pushed the boat into the narrow creek using one oar to push on the creek bottom. Everyone called the creek, Crab Creek. It had been the best place to crab since I was a boy—and that was 40 years from the date of the story.

"Why is Crab Creek the best place to catch crabs?" Polly asked. An innocent question is usually the best start for a memorable Air Snake.

"The Tongue of the Tide brings crabs straight here," I told Polly.

"What's the Tongue of the Tide?" she asked.

"When the tide changes from low tide to high tide, it changes way out in the ocean, then the incoming tide surges up the Savannah River," I carefully explained.

"And right on the surge of the tide is where most of the crabs ride into the rivers and creeks." I kept making up the story and Polly kept believing me. "The edge of the new tide is called the Tongue of the Tide."

Polly's serious face told me she bought the story hook, line, and sinker. So, I continued,

"The tongue of the tide is the leading edge of the incoming tide, and the crabs, shrimp, and fish are swept along in its current."

I waited a few seconds. She didn't rebuke me or laugh at me. She asked,

"So, what then?"

"The Tongue of the Tide sweeps from the Savannah River into the Wilmington River only in Wilmington because it is a natural fork and the leading edge of the tide follows the least resistance." That part of the story is true; there was a natural fork where the Wilmington River flowed round a bend into the Savannah River.

I waited... then continued.

"The Tongue of the Tide sweeps into the Herb River and then into

Crab Creek." I explained there was a natural fork at each intersection. I was proud of my story, so I added, "Like an arrow going to a target, the Tongue of the Tide brings more crabs right here into Crab Creek than any other creek around here. To establish credibility, I kept looking at my crab line in the water. If I looked at Polly, I'd have laughed.

"The Tongue of the Tide sweeps all the crabs from the Ocean right into Crab Creek." I finished. The credibility of this story was the fact that everyone knew there were more crabs in Crab Creek than any other place in Bonna Bella.

I said nothing to the contrary. When we had a basket full of crabs, I used the oar to push my way out of Crab Creek and rowed back to return the boat. I was tempted to tell Polly and Ruth the truth there at the dock, but I decided to wait for a better place to explain that the Tongue of the Tide was an Air Snake. I wanted to get the maximum results. We went home and cooked the crabs in a pot over a small wood fire in the backyard. When we were sitting around the picnic table that would have been a good time to tell the family, but I didn't.

What makes my Air Snakes credible is that eventually I have to tell the family where I misled them. I have never let my family go on believing an Air Snake forever. That would make it a lie. Shortly after telling an Air Snake, I've always told them the truth. About midnight that night, Ruth and I were in bed. She had already turned over and I could tell by her deep breathing she was almost asleep. Then I whispered gently in her ear.

"The Tongue of the Tide is an Air Snake."

"WHAT!!" She sat up in bed like a firecracker had exploded in the room. It wasn't a firecracker exploding, it was her.

"WHAT!!" She continued to yell.

"You'll wake the kids," I tried to lower her voice.

"I SURE WILL WAKE THE KIDS!!" Her voice was now heard throughout the house.

"POLLY!" Ruth yelled.

"THE TONGUE OF THE TIDE IS AN AIR SNAKE!" She announced into the next room and for everyone in the house to hear.

To this day, the kids remember the Tongue of the Tide better than all the other fabricated stories. Debbie wanted to write a book about Air Snakes and title it *Lies My Father Told Me.*

Sam likes to repeat the Air Snake that happened to him the first time I took him to Wrigley Field to see the Chicago Cubs play ball. We were sitting behind home plate, when the bottom of the seventh inning approached. I told him,

"When I stand up everyone will stand with me..."

"Oh-h-h-h," he didn't know what to say.

"I'll get everyone to stand up with me" I told him. So as soon as the last out was made in the top of the seventh inning, I jumped to my feet; waved my arms for people to get up and yelled.

"EVERYBODY UP!!"

To Sam's amazement, the entire ballpark began standing. Everyone!!

"Oh-h-h-h ..." was all I heard Sam say.

Later I explained the meaning of the seventh inning stretch. And like a chip off the old block, now he's done the same thing to others. He jumps to his feet and motions others to get up.

To this day, when I begin an Air Snake, my wife and children (now approximately age 40) begin waving their hands in the air like an Air Snake gliding in the breeze from the tall bushes.

PRINCIPLES TO TAKE AWAY

1. The Truth Telling Principle. Your children must know that

you are committed to telling the truth. It begins by your example. When you tell the truth and it hurts or it costs you, they will know your commitment to truth. They must learn that you expect them to tell the truth, because you tell the truth, and you will punish them for lies. But when it comes to "Little Jack Horner," or *Huckleberry Finn*, or *The Princess Bride*, these stories have their place for enjoyment. You may tell your children about Santa Claus as though he is real, when you know he's fictitious. You won't harm them, nor blunt their growth.

2. <u>The Principle of Developing Discernment</u>. I didn't want my children to be gullible when they grew up. I wanted them to be able to discern who was telling the truth and who was leading them astray. So, I told them about Air Snakes to help them become discerning.

As I grew up in the south, my uncles told me, "tall tales." Some of these helped to develop my creativity. Others gave me a sober opinion of the truth.

As a small boy my uncles told me tall tales, then laughed at me when they "caught" me in childish naivety. Once Uncle Gene sent me to pick some small hot peppers out of the garden. He told me small hot peppers were not as hot as large hot peppers. Then he told me the faster I ate one, the less it would burn my mouth. The opposite was true on both occasions! Smaller hot peppers are MUCH hotter, and slower is better. Then Uncle Gene offered me a penny if I'd eat a small one fast . . . real fast. I wanted the penny, so I gulped it down, and burned my mouth, throat and stomach. Uncle Gene and the other men all laughed. I decided my children wouldn't be naive, nor gullible as I had been as a child. I also decided I would not embarrass my children as I had been embarrassed. Once I got them to believe about Air Snakes, I never laughed at them nor humiliated them, as my uncle had done to me.

3. <u>The Principle That Stories Are Fun</u>. I taught my children we could live in all kinds of worlds without being there. We could learn something from every situation and have fun doing it. It's easier to stay on the path of life if you tell your children a laughable story that will

keep them on the straight and narrow. Too often we fuss at children for walking too close to the edge where they will hurt themselves. Why is it that the more we fuss, the more they rebel? Why is it that the more commands we give them, the closer to the edge they wander? So, Air Snake stories taught them to walk in the center of the path of life.

> **That which is learned and enjoyed,**
>
> **is retained.**
>
> **That which is hated when taught,**
>
> **is forgotten.**

4. <u>The Principle of Harmless Illustrations</u>. Air Snakes are not real, no one has ever been bitten by an Air Snake. I say in a joking way, "no one has ever died from them." I doubt if anyone became a killer by hearing about the *Three Little Pigs* boiling the wolf to death. Children see the obvious point of the stories and overlook the marginal incidents that are needed to give reality to the story.

5. <u>The Vicarious Identification Principle</u>. Stories transport us to another time and place. They allow us to live in another world. When our present conditions are agonizing, a story helps us to vicariously assume the happiness of others. A story helps children experience the consequences of transgression and maybe keeps them from hurting themselves.

Everyone wants improvement, and stories give us hope, i.e. life will get better. And through stories, the dreams we desire, help us endure the failure we experience. Stories don't just tell us of a better life, they make our life better.

CHAPTER TWO

MAKING BOOKS:
CAN WE HAVE MCDONALD'S?

The first book that I wrote and published was *Teaching Teens*, a book I self-published. I was a professor of Christian Education at Midwest Bible College in downtown St. Louis, Missouri. The college is located in a large old church building that had an auditorium seating 2,000, plus classrooms located in three or four large Victorian homes. In the fall of 1959, I was teaching Christian Education of Youth, and there was no adequate textbook on how to organize a church youth group program from an evangelical point of view. My students were reading a YMCA published book, and from other books on youth work written from a mainline orientation.

I decided to write my own textbook from a biblical orientation. Since I had already taught the course the previous year, I had a fairly good set of notes. So, I assigned each student in the class to write up one section of my notes as a chapter of this book. I decided to call it *Teaching Teens*. As each chapter/term paper was submitted, I edited them to make the material say what I was trying to teach in class.

One student was assigned the task of typing the entire manuscript onto mimeograph stencils. For those who are young and don't remember, a mimeograph stencil was soft paper that was wrapped around a large ink blackened drum. Office printing was called mimeographing, long before the day of xeroxing, faxing, or any type of modern-day copying machine.

My students and I all gathered at the college for an evening of pizza and work. We used an old-fashioned mimeograph machine, so it had to be hand cranked to turn out printed sheets. The book we were creating had 84 pages, so we printed one hundred copies of each page. This meant we were printing 100 books. As soon as one student printed 100 pages another student punched holes in the sheets for spiral binding. Another student began correlating the pages in order. We worked past midnight but put together 100 copies of an eighty-four-page book with a nice, crisp blue cardboard cover that announced to the world, *Teaching Teens*, by Elmer Towns.

Everyone in class got two or three copies, we sold others for five dollars each throughout the student body. My class sponsored a youth seminar and sold copies of the book to church workers. We didn't make any money, but we earned enough to buy pizza for the class two or three times, plus cover all of our cost of paper, ink and stencils.

I kept the stencils knowing that in the future I would want to use them for a second printing of the book. I began thinking about selling *Teaching Teens* to earn money. I was constantly broke.

Midwest Bible College was a faith institution, which meant the college trusted God for money to pay for expenses and faculty salary. If enough money was donated to the college, the faculty were paid. When money did not come in, faculty were only paid part of their salary. So, there were some occasions when I only got half of my salary, some occasions only 10 percent, and those unhappy occasions when I was not paid at all. I felt that a faculty member in a Bible college should not flip hamburgers at a greasy spoon, nor should a faculty member go out early every morning delivering papers for a living. I trusted God to take care of all of my needs. After I saw how easy it was to sell *Teaching Teens*, I saw potential where I could earn extra money selling *Teaching Teens* in church meetings.

One evening I brought home the mimeograph from the college, set it up on the ping-pong table in the basement, and spent the larger part of the evening, past midnight, printing 84 pages of *Teaching Teens*.

Making Books: Can We Have McDonald's?

The next evening, I brought home the machines to perforate holes for the spiral binding. Again, it took me past midnight to punch holes in all the pages.

The following weekend I had to go speak to a Sunday school teachers meeting in a local church. I had eighty-four piles of paper; each pile represented a page in my book. This is where my kids come in. Actually, it involved Debbie who was five and Sam who was four years old. Polly was too young to get involved in putting the book together.

We collated the book. Each of us walked around the basement, picking up one page at a time, each putting together one book. We began by the basement stairs, walking clockwise around the basement, picking up pages of the book off the ping-pong table, the washing machine, the dryer, an old chair, anything that would hold paper.

"Come on kids and help me," I said to Debbie and Sam.

"Do we hafta?" Debbie said, which is the usual reaction of children.

I realized to motivate her properly I had to appeal to her interest. So, I said to Debbie, "If you help me gather the pages of my book," I reasoned with her young mind, "I'll sell these books to get enough money for McDonald's."

"YEAH!" She was ready to help.

"YEAH," agreed Sam.

So, we all lined up from the ping-pong table, to the washing machine, to the dryer, to the folding chair, around the room each of us walked, putting the book together. Then I inserted the pages into the spiraling machine to bind them into a book. I took seven copies with me to a Sunday school teacher's meeting where I spoke. If I could sell them all, that was thirty-five dollars. In those days our total grocery bill was approximately fifteen to twenty dollars a week.

That first evening I sold three copies of *Teaching Teens*, making $15.00. While $15.00 is not much today, I saw a way to provide for my family. In addition, the church gave me $5.00 for speaking to the Sunday school teachers. On the way home I went by the grocery store buying all of the basic necessities that our family needed for the week, and then stopped by McDonald's to get the hamburgers, French fries and cokes I had promised the kids.

My kids have always worked hard, and their employers have been happy with them. Maybe it's because early they developed a work ethic. I involved them in making money that brought home groceries and other necessities. They usually didn't beg for McDonald's, because they knew that they had to do something to get a "treat."

"Daddy, could we go downstairs to put together some books," Debbie said to me one day. She wanted the family to go to McDonald's, and she knew we didn't have the money. But she also knew that when I got money from selling books, we went to McDonald's. But I had to tell her,

"I'm not speaking tonight, so I can't sell any books."

Some children or wives of ministers complain when father goes off for ministry, my kids were always supportive of my speaking and ministry. They knew that when I went to preach, they would get the benefit of my ministry.

During the Christmas season of 1960 I was invited to deliver the Christmas Banquet sermon for First Baptist Church, Grafton, Illinois where Rev. William Blake was pastor. Blake was a graduate of the college where I taught and knew how tight it was financially for the faculty. After the banquet was over, he handed me an envelope saying,

"I know money is tight for you, because you don't always get your paycheck," Blake explained that he was supportive of what I did. Blake told me,

"So, my church and I want to give you an extra offering." I expected five or ten dollars for speaking at the banquet and would have been very happy with that. I would probably have taken the ten dollars and stopped by the grocery store on the way home, buying the basic necessities we needed for the week. But Rev. Blake handed me the check and said, "Go ahead, look in it."

Opening it, I saw that it was for twenty-five dollars, which was more that twice what I had expected.

On the way home I approached the Chain of Rocks Bridge over the Mississippi River taking me from Illinois into St. Louis, Missouri. On the north side of the road was an old tumbled down shed called, "Grandpa's," It was nothing but a large shed with a dirt floor where they sold vegetables in the summertime, apples in the fall, and during the Christmas season they sold toys at cheap discount prices.

I walked into "Grandpa's" and saw three things that I wanted to buy for my children.

The first thing I saw was a large riding toy. It was a yellow tractor with pedals. The wheels resembled tractor wheels. "That's for Polly," I thought.

Next, I saw a red fire engine with wooden ladders, and a little string attached to the bell on the front. It was for Sam. He could climb inside and pedal to make it go.

Finally, I saw a scat car for Debbie. A scat car is simply a frame of a car without fenders, hood or any other attachments just the frame or wheel and a steering wheel. The scat car was pedal powered and because it was built so low to the ground, it would whip around the sidewalk corner faster than the tractor or fire truck. They might tip over.

"How much for the children's riding toys?" I asked the man in his late 20s. Obviously, he was not a grandpa or related to a grandpa. "Grandpa's" was just a name that they called the place.

"Eight dollars a piece," his answer.

"Wow," I said, "they cost twice that much at Famous Barr or Sears and Roebuck."

"Yep..."

"I'd like to get them," I reasoned with the man, "but I don't have cash."

"That's too bad."

"But I do have a check," I explained to the young man behind the counter. "I spoke tonight at the First Baptist Church in Grafton, Illinois, for their Christmas banquet and they gave me this check."

I showed him the check for $25.00. Then I told him I could only buy two, I had to keep $10.00 for groceries. I began looking at the three riding toys, the yellow truck, the red fire engine and the scat car.

"WHICH TWO WILL I TAKE," I asked myself.

I had already decided that Polly would get the yellow tractor, Sam would get the red fire engine and Debbie would get the scat car. So, which two kids get something and, which one gets left out. That was a tough decision and I was taking a long time to make up my mind. I was happy to bring toys home, and I was happy to give all the money I made to the kids, but I was not happy to pick two out of three.

"Which two will it be?" The salesman came back to talk with me. He could see I was having difficulty making up my mind. It's hard to choose against one child.

"Tell you what I'll do ..." the surrogate Grandpa said. "I'll give ya all three for fifteen bucks."

"Amen," I blurted out.

"Yep," he understood what amen meant.

I drove home a happy "Santa Claus" because I would make my kids happy, and I even had enough for groceries. I realized God sometimes supplied our need through a salary check, sometimes from the sale of *Teaching Teens*, and sometimes by honorarium from speaking. But that evening, God moved Rev. Blake to give a larger honorarium than most, and God moved a man at Grandpa's to give me three riding toys for $15.00. Raising my children, I relied on the Scripture, "Our God shall supply all your needs," (Phil. 4:19).

He did in many ways.

PRINCIPLES TO TAKE AWAY

1. The principle that we get identity from our work. The opposite in also true, working effectively gives us our identity. I wanted to be a teacher yet didn't make enough money to meet our physical needs for my salary. I was not embarrassed to cook hamburgers, nor was I too lazy to work a secular job. It's just that I wanted to serve the Lord wholeheartedly, not part time. I was not against physical work because I helped paint the buildings of Midwest Bible College. I did what others wouldn't do, I climbed the scaffolds to paint eaves and gables of rooftops. But that physical labor gave meaning to my life, for I was serving God with the lectures and the ladder.

I got an obvious identification out of writing textbooks and have continued to do so throughout my life. I wrote them, hand cranked the manuscript machine and perforated the pages. My kids identified with "making books" and it was a way God provided for our needs.

2. The principle of learning by doing. Some things in life are only learned by involvement. You can't learn to swim by reading a book and a pitcher can't develop a curve ball watching a film. Perfection in learning takes involvement practice and commitment. I felt the best was to teach youth about youth work was to involve them in a project. They helped to write a book, type the chapters, then print and assemble the first project. Then they helped plan and sponsor a youth seminar on doing youth ministry.

3. The principle of God's supply from unexpected sources. When I didn't get my salary from Midwest Bible College, God supplied through various sources. When preaching at churches, I received an honorarium and sometimes individuals gave me gifts. There was one family who showed up at our home with racks of groceries on several

occasions. Also, I sold copies of *Teaching Teens*. God was always faithful to supply our needs.

4. The principle of work appreciation. We appreciate the things for which we work. I taught my children to work so they could get McDonald's, and they developed appreciation for the labor I gave to the ministry, as well as what they had to do to get an award. I believe if we teach our kids to "work for what they love," eventually they will learn to, "love their work."

5. The dignity of work principle. The work of God is not just preaching, teaching, praying and winning souls. The work of God involves dirty, hard work, which may mean we get our hands black with printing ink from a mimeograph. The work of God involves sweat work which involves turning the crank of a machine past midnight to print a book. When my kids had to monotonously walk around the basement to assemble a book, the fact that the book had Christian contact didn't sanctify the process. Whatsoever we do, we are commanded to do all to the glory of God. I tried to elevate children to see that their work, and mine, had implications. Because we worked, God's work went forward, and because we worked, we got rewarded immediately. We went to McDonald's.

CHAPTER THREE

THE CUBS:
YA GOTTA ROOT FOR SOMEONE

"I'm home," I yelled, walking in the front door of our home in Deerfield, Illinois. "What's for lunch?" I asked Ruth who was busy fixing lunch in the kitchen. The clock on the kitchen wall said 11:55 AM. "THE KIDS WILL BE HERE SOON," I thought.

It was May 8, 1966, the 10th birthday of my son, Sam. I knew what day it was, and I knew Ruth was fixing his favorite dinner. When I asked about lunch, she said,

"Hamburgers..., Sam's favorite," and then she thought for a moment and added, "mashed potatoes... you know he loves mashed potatoes."

The kids went to three different schools in three different directions, and we lived in the middle of them. It was not more than three blocks to any one of the schools, so they came home for lunch.

Sitting in my usual spot at the head of the table, I glanced over the sports page of the newspaper waiting for the kids to get home for lunch. Then I saw that the Cubs had a day game at 2:00 pm.

"H-m-m-m-m-m," I thought to myself. "I'd like to see that game, but I don't have anyone to go with me."

"I oughta take Sam," I thought, but there were problems.

I had attended school for twelve years, grade one through high school graduation and never cut a class. I expected the same rigid attendance policy of my children. I did the same in college, I never cut a class there because perfect attendance was a badge of spirituality. However, seminary allowed a certain quota of cuts, so my attendance was not perfect.

"Should I let Sam cut this afternoon," the thought went through my mind. I was debating a moral issue. Should I make my son go to school to have a perfect record, or should I take him to a baseball game for his birthday.

"What would Ruth think?" I wondered if my wife would approve of Sam missing school, so I said nothing but continued to think about it.

After the kids got home for lunch, we all had hamburgers and mashed potatoes and I began a slow interrogation of my son.

"Do you have any tests this afternoon?"

"No."

"Do you have to give a report or be there for any special project?"

"No."

"Anything special going on this afternoon?"

"No-o-o-o-o-o-o-o," Sam let the answer slowly flow out of his mouth. He knew something was in the air.

Ruth looked down at the end of the table, she also knew something was in the air. Her eye had that special glint that meant she knew what I was thinking. She was not as rigid in attendance as I was.

Our eyes met, and I knew she approved of what I was thinking, even though I didn't tell her what was on my mind.

"We used to live in St. Louis," I explained to Sam, "and we rooted for the St. Louis Cardinals." I went on to explain to him that each time we went back to visit his Uncle Burt, we always went to Busch Stadium to see the St. Louis Cardinals to play ball. "We were Cardinal fans."

When we left St. Louis we moved to Winnipeg, Canada, where there was not a major league team. Even in Canada, we rooted for the Cardinals. Radio station KMOX from St. Louis had a clear channel, and late at night we could pick up Harry Carey broadcasting the St. Louis Cardinals way up in Canada. So, we were St. Louis Cardinal fans, even though we were distant fans.

"If we're going to live in Chicago," I explained to Sam, "we ought to root for a Chicago team."

Sam didn't say anything, but he nodded his head in approval.

"I don't think we ought to root for the White Sox," I continued my analysis. "The White Sox are way down on the Southside and we live on the North side." Everyone knew that people living on the Southside of Chicago usually rooted for the White Sox, while people on the North side rooted for the Cubs.

"Let's just make a decision to root for the Cubs," I squinted my eyes and looked to Sam for a response.

"What's wrong with the White Sox?" my son asked.

"Rooting for the White Sox is about as much fun as watching paint dry," I explained that the Southside team was boring.

"The Cubs never win," Ruth said, even though she was not a baseball fan she knew the reputation of the Cubs. She explained, "Everybody in American knows the Cubs are not winners, if anything they are losers."

"They need us," I explained to the family. That's all the more reason to root for them." Then I turned to Sam announcing, "I've got a great idea!" I said to him.

"What?"

"Why don't you cut school this afternoon and let's go see a Cub's game?"

"Let's go ..."

There was no discussion about truancy, or a negative impact on our son's academic achievement. It was an instant decision we made sitting around the dining room table.

I looked at my wallet and had enough money to cover the price of the tickets. Within two minutes we were in the Chevy Impala, backing out of the driveway heading for Wrigley Field.

In the summer of 1966, the Cubs were pathetic but there was something lovable about the inept Cubs. Sam and I went on his birthday, and for the next five years, we always went to the Cubs' game on his birthday. Usually between 2 thousand to 4 thousand people attended a home game, and we could have just about any seat at Wrigley Stadium we wanted.

Baseball is not American until you go to an old stadium, one like Wrigley Field, built before World War I where the smell of beer and peanuts seeped into the concrete. No matter how many rainstorms washed the grandstands, it smelled like a baseball stadium. It smelled like beer and peanuts. It's a smell you hate to love because it always beer and peanuts.

Wrigley Field had grass, real grass! Unlike the artificial grass of the Astrodome and the other new stadiums that were being built.

Wrigley Field had bleacher bums, idiots who stripped to the waist, painted themselves red, white and blue and did audacious things to attract attention. Also, there were businessmen who stripped to the waist to get a suntan while watching an afternoon game.

Wrigley Field did not have lights, it had God's sunlight, and in the late afternoon the sun came over the third base and blinded the right fielder, making a normal catch a theatric experience.

The Cubs: Ya Gotta Root For Someone

And what other stadium has real green ivy growing on the walls, not plastic ivy like you would buy at K-Mart but real ivy. In the early spring the ivy was brown during the first games of April and May and turned green with the sun and rain of the late spring and summer.

Wrigley Field has Cracker Jacks, peanuts, and hot dogs; but Sam and I love Polish sausage. A Polish sausage was about the size of a hotdog, with mustard, relish and ketchup, it was ten times better than a hotdog. Wrigley Stadium had little stoves on wheels that were pushed through the grandstand. No one could resist the smell of frying Polish sausage right under your nose. We spent more money on Polish sausages than we did on tickets.

For the next five years, the Cubs had a home stand during the first week of May, always on Sam's birthday. Those were formative days in my son's life, and I use tradition to build expectation in him. Two or three days before his birthday I would check the Cubs' schedule, and sure enough they were playing on his birthday. On the morning of his birthday, I never told him what we were going to do. Sam always wondered, but never asked. He always came home for lunch, Ruth always had hamburgers and mashed potatoes. Each year we would get to the end of the meal and then I would say something like "what do you think?"

"Do you think we ought to go to see the Cubs?"

"Sure."

"Let's do it."

"Let's go now."

And within two minutes we were out the front door, in the Chevy Impala, on our way to Wrigley Field. Sam and I watched the Cubs on Channel 9 television, it was unlike any other television station in the world. When you watched WGN Channel 9, it was like a yellow hound dog sitting by your easy chair, WGN was friendly and comfortable.

The announcer for the Cubs in those days was Jack Brickhouse. Every time Ernie Banks, or Randy Hundley hit a home run, he would yell,

"Hey, hey ..."

As Sam grew into manhood, he continued to root for the Cubs, even though we moved to Virginia, Georgia, and then back to Virginia. As soon as cable television came into our homes, we ordered WGN and continued our love affair with the Cubs.

Each spring I stand before my Sunday school class at Thomas Road Baptist Church and announce to the world through radio, television and the live audience that,

"This is the year the Cubs are going to win the World Series ..."

Each year I am wrong for the Cubs have never won the World Series since we've been fans. My son cautions me each year,

"Be careful, Dad, ..." his wisdom exceeds his age, "the Cubs are a team you hate to love ... because eventually they'll break your heart."

"He's right!"

But there was one eventual day in the summer of 1969 we still talk about. It was the day we got to go down and walk on the playing field of Wrigley Stadium. It was a day we never forgot.

Manager Leo Durocher had taken over the helm of the Cubs and directed them into first place. Rather than 2000 through 4000 in attendance, Wrigley Field was crowded. We had to get there early to get a seat. There was Cub Fever on the corner of Addison and Clark, the Cubs were in first place and everyone smelled a World Series.

The memorable event happened on another day, not Sam's birthday. I came home for lunch to find Tim Hoefling and a couple of other boys eating lunch around the table with Sam. I took my usual chair at the head of the table and was glancing over the sports page, noticing a game against the St. Louis Cardinals at 2:00 PM.

The Cubs: Ya Gotta Root For Someone

"Cardinals are playing the Cubs today," I told the boys, "I ought to go to that game ..." Letting my words trail off into nothing, I looked around the table. Suddenly, all four boys stopped talking. With wide boyish grins, they looked at me in anticipation.

"Anybody want to go to the game with me?" I threw the question out casually.

Four boys immediately stuck up a hand and yelled, "Yea-a-a-a-a." Then to make it emphatic, they put up two hands.

"Let's do it!"

Within two minutes we were out the front door in the Chevy Impala, heading for Wrigley Field.

Because the Cubs were in first place, many fans that I called "Johnny Come Latelies" had flocked Addison and Clark, taking up the best parking places. I had learned that we had to park approximately six blocks away when I saw the first sign of traffic congestion. On this particular day, at about six blocks away; there was no crowd.

"Strange ...," I said to the boys, "there's no crowd for the game." Then we got to within four blocks from Wrigley Field. Still there was no crowd. This really dumbfounded me.

"This is really strange ...," my additional commentary.

We kept driving until we saw the famous Cubs sign at Wrigley Field and to our amazement, the spaces for players and staff right in front of Wrigley Field were empty. No one was there. There was no crowd. The ticket windows were closed. There were no concessionaires anywhere. It was a normal workday and only a few people were walking down Addison Street in front of Wrigley Field.

I had read yesterday's newspaper, that read the Cubs were playing the Cardinals in Chicago. But today they were playing the Astros in Houston.

I sat at the stop light on the corner of Addison and Clark, not knowing what to do. The light changed green, and there was no one behind me honking a horn. There was no traffic to stop me, when a brilliant thought hit me. I pulled across the street and parked in a spot marked for "Player."

"Why not?" I said to the boys.

"Yeah, yeah!!!"

"Let's go!" I instructed them to get out and lock the car.

"Where are we going?" Sam asked.

"Would you like to walk on out to the infield grass of Wrigley Field?" I asked.

I saw little boys' eyes get absolutely wild in anticipation.

"Do you mean we can ...?" They couldn't even finish the sentence.

"Yeah ..."

The gate was open, and we walked right in as if we had an invitation. A woman met us walking through the runway, but she didn't stop us. She must have been an office worker. She turned toward the concession stands and headed up the hallway. She didn't speak to us, we didn't speak to her; and luckily she didn't ask what we were doing.

Then out of the tunnel we walked out into the sunlight, right into the middle of the grandstand, directly behind home plate. We stopped to take it all in, the green folding seats, the protective mesh wire to keep foul balls from flying back into the crowd. We look up where the radio announcers sat.

"Follow me, guys!" I said heading down toward the third base gate. There was a small gate leading onto the field, and it was open. To me, an open gate was an invitation, so I obliged.

We stepped out of the grandstand onto the playing field, and one of the Hoefling boys dropped to his knees and began rubbing the grass with the palm of his hands.

"This is real grass."

"You guys had better quickly run the bases," I instructed them. I knew that it wouldn't be long before we would be kicked off the infield.

"The bases are not there," I noticed, "can you pretend where they are?" I asked.

"Yeah," the boys yelled as they broke into a dead run. Tim the oldest quickly outdistanced the others. They started running down to where first base ought to be located.

"HEY," yelled one of the groundkeepers who finally spotted the boys between second and third base.

"GET OFF THE INFIELD," he yelled at the top of his voice. And then looking at me, he yelled again,

"GET THOSE KIDS OUTTA HERE!"

He said a few other things, but I don't remember what they are, and being a minister of the Gospel, I probably shouldn't remember what they are. But I did yell back to him,

"I wanted to give the boys a thrill ..."

"BUT THEY'RE NOT ALLOWED ON THE FIELD," the groundskeeper's loud voice could be heard all over Wrigley Stadium.

Later I learned a principle from Jerry Falwell, "It's easier to get forgiveness than permission." As I led the boys off Wrigley Field, I realized that if I had asked permission to go on to the field, they would never have granted it. We just did it and we now have a lifetime memory. We were not arrested, nor did they physically throw us off the field. The groundskeeper didn't say anything else as we left. I guess we were forgiven.

Every once in awhile when Sam and I are watching a Cubs game, we point to a spot on the infield between home plate and the Cubs' dugout. We talk about standing there one day in 1969 when I took four boys to see a Cubs game, but it was the wrong day.

PRINCIPLES TO TAKE AWAY

1. <u>The principle that sports develops character</u>. The physical education teacher or the coach is one of the most important faculty members on a school staff. While academic people tend to look down their scholarly nose at athletes for its lack of academic content, many children develop character by playing sports. When children are a part of a team, they develop a will to win, and a will to excel.

Sports can lead to academic excellence, if they learn to be a winner in every area of their lives. Also, sports teaches children self-discipline and playing by the rules, a necessary ingredient to learning character, i.e. habitually doing the right thing in the right way. Playing on a sports team also develops an attitude of teamwork. Children must depend upon someone else to get a hit to drive them in from second base, or to make a tackle on the other side of the field so they can win. In teamwork children learn to trust one another, to depend on one another, and to respect one another. And a team usually loses when they argue because of arrogance or stupidity. So, when your children play on a team, they learn some of the most important contributions that a school can offer to them.

But competition also teaches them how to properly lose in life, for in an imperfect world and when dealing with imperfect people, we sometimes lose. We forget the plays, we strike out, or we just "blow it." And learning to lose graciously, is just as important as learning to win humbly.

P.S. Anyone who roots for the Cubs is an expert at anticipation.

2. <u>The principle of anticipation</u>. For six years on his birthday, I took Sam to see the Cubs play an afternoon game. Family traditions are good because they teach anticipation and give value to the future. Letting Sam "skip" school to go to a baseball game became one of

those defining events of his life, just as important as teaching him school punctuality and faithfulness.

But other aspects of anticipation were taught through our love affair with the Cubs. Each year we anticipated them to win, and each year they somehow "dropped the ball." Because each year when I say I will never watch them again, the following spring I renew my love affair with the Cubs.

3. <u>The principle of deciding to be loyal</u>. How does a child develop loyalty in a team, or to a hero, or to any other cause? Sometimes they develop loyalty because of a hero worship, and at other times loyalty grows because of our children's closeness or proximity, they are loyal to those close to them. On May 8, 1966, Sam and I made a decision to be loyal to the Cubs, and over thirty years later we still root for them. To examine loyalty carefully, a decision produced loyalty, and then our relationship to the Cubs produced ongoing decisions of more loyalty. We decided to no longer root for the Cardinals, but we decided to root for the Cubs. We began going to the games and we became loyal to the Cubs. We made many other decisions based on that original decision. We decided to buy cable television to see the Cubs play, and we visit Chicago annually to visit Wrigley Field. The same principle applies to building loyalty to a church. We teach our children to loyally attend church, which means we must make a decision to support a local church by joining it, paying tithes to it, and serving the Lord in that church. After we begin attending a local church, we find that we like the people there and we receive many benefits from the church. So, our loyalty to the church produces many other decisions, such as helping out as an usher, inviting our friends, or by being loyal to its services.

PARTING ADVICE

Be careful of following my advice to root for the Cubs. They are a team you hate to love because eventually they will break your heart.

CHAPTER FOUR

THE CAMERA AND BALL GLOVE: LEARNING HONESTY

"Look Daddy." Debbie came running down the hall, "I found a camera." She held out an expensive 35mm camera with a 50mm lens. "How much does it cost?" she asked.

I held out my hand to examine it. A half a roll of unexposed film was still in the camera. When looking through the lens, I knew Debbie had found an expensive one.

"Over $150.00," I told her.

"Mine's better than yours," she was giddy with her new prize. My camera at home was much cheaper than this one.

"Where did you find it?" I asked. "We've got to locate the owner."

Debbie and I rushed down a hall to the bench where the camera was found. No one was there. . . no one was looking around like they might be looking for a lost camera. She had found the camera on a long low bench without a back, located in a back hallway of the Chicago Museum of Science and Arts.

"Let's try to find the owner" I had a high degree of ownership, and I wanted my children to have that same attitude toward the possessions of others. I told Debbie to hang the camera on her shoulder and to walk a distance from me. I was going to ask people if they lost a camera. They would have to describe it to get it. I didn't want anyone to claim the camera by describing what they saw in Debbie's hand. Then with Debbie standing a distance away I began asking everyone.

"Did you lose a camera?"

"Yes" the first man told me. He quickly added, "Thanks... I misplaced it just a little while ago."

"What brand was it?" I asked.

"Polaroid," he answered after thinking about it.

"Sorry..." I told him and walked away.

He was not the only one who tried to claim the camera. Others said they too lost a camera, but none of their descriptions of their apparent lost cameras matched the one Debbie found.

"Let's check the Lost and Found." I told Debbie. Again, no one had reported losing a camera. There were no names left by distraught camera owners.

As we walked through the museum, Debbie kept her distance from me. I kept asking guards and concession salesmen.

"Did anyone tell you they lost a camera?"

"No."

Finally, it was time to go home. I didn't want to take someone's camera home.

"What are we going to do?" Debbie asked.

We questioned the attendant at the Lost and Found room, still no one reported a lost camera. So, I turned over the camera to the attendant and gave him my name and address, including my phone number.

He wrote down correctly everything I told him; I had checked to make sure he wrote it down right. Then I included a note in the camera case.

"This camera was found by my daughter. I wanted to teach her a lesson in honesty. It would be nice if you sent her a dollar reward. Mail to Debbie Towns."

As my family drove away from the Chicago Museum of Science and Industry, I felt reinforced that I had done the right thing, we had to be honest.

Two days later I phoned the museum, asking to speak to the attendant in charge of Lost and Found. I identified myself as the father of the girl who found the camera. I didn't get the same attendant who had received the camera. It was a much older voice.

"Has someone claimed the camera?" I asked.

I described, the camera and told him how expensive it was. I told how I carefully wrote down my name and address so we could retrieve the camera if no one claimed it.

"Let me check the records," the gruff voice sounded like it was chewing a cigar. "We don't got no record of any camera received dis week."

"I left the camera two days ago" I protested. "I wrote my name and address on the receipt book."

"Not here Mac..." was the only answer I got.

"Let me speak to the supervisor."

"You's got me Mack," I felt he was laughing at me through the phone.

"I'm da supervisor" he told me. He explained in typical Southside Chicago slang who might have taken the camera and destroyed the records I had left.

"It could be 30 or 40 kids in this office... they all work Lost and Found." Then he consoled me,

"The camera's gone."

We discussed the matter around our family dinner table. This was the place where we reviewed the events of the day. It was where I did a lot of teaching.

"You could have had a great camera," I told Debbie, "but you didn't have one before you went to the museum, so it's not as though you lost a personal camera. You never had it."

"We lost the camera," I told the kids. "What can we learn?" I asked, "How will we handle it next time."

Ruth suggested a plan - a good plan. Her plan would protect the owner of the lost property and if possible, get the item back to the owner. But Ruth's plan also protected our children if they found an item. Her plan provided how the child could keep the found treasure yet remain honest.

Next summer we had an opportunity to put Ruth's plan into action.

We were on Jekyll Island, one of the barrier islands off the coast of Georgia for a family vacation. They are also called the Golden Isles of Georgia because the marsh grass turns golden brown in the wintertime. We had rented a recreational trailer in Savannah, Georgia and we were planning a trip to Florida. Jekyll Island is only 80 miles from Savannah, so that was one first night's stop. We set up the trailer and went swimming in the ocean about sunset. Sam and I took a walk down the beach looking for some shells in the shallow water.

Sam saw an almost new baseball glove. He ran to pick it up. No one was around, there was no owner.

The Camera And Ball Glove: Learning Honesty

"Wow," Sam said, "just what I've always wanted."

"We have to find the owner," I replied.

Looking up and down the beach we saw only a few people walking a distance away. They didn't look like ball players. They looked more like strollers than athletes. Sam hid the glove under a towel, and we stopped people in sight to ask if they'd lost a baseball glove.

No one claimed it.

Down the beach was a lone lifeguard, perched on a high lifeguard chair. Both feet were curled under him as he stared out at the ocean. He was about ready to go home.

"Anybody report a lost ball glove?" I yelled up to him.

"Nope..." he shook his head negatively, "not today."

"We found one" I pointed to my son, indicating he actually found it.

"I'll keep it for the owner" the lifeguard reached down as if I would give it to him. But I remember a Lost and Found attendant at the museum who had kept the camera.

"No," I said. "I want to give it to the owner myself."

I told the lifeguard my name and instructed him that we would give the glove to the person who was able to identify it.

"We're over in the trailer park," I pointed toward a grove of low oak trees, all bent by the prevailing ocean winds. "We're parked in the first space," I instructed him. "If anyone asks for a lost glove, send them over for it.

That evening we drove off the island for some ice cream. On the way out I spotted the ranger station where people registered their trailer. It was a state park. I took Sam into the office with me. We greeted the ranger, and I spoke to my son.

I wanted him to learn how to handle responsible negotiations. "Sam, you tell the ranger what happened."

Sam spoke right up, "I found a baseball glove," he explained. " I just want to make sure it gets to the owner who lost it."

Sam explained where our trailer was parked and filled out a piece of paper giving our trailer space. Then he added, "I'll put my address in Chicago so they can write for it." But he still remembered the camera. "They'll have to describe the glove to get it."

"The lifeguard wanted us to give the glove to him," Sam added his interpretation of the lifeguard's motive. "But I bet he would have kept it."

I had to explain to the ranger how we found a camera in the Chicago's Museum of Science and Industry. While I was telling what happened, Sam interrupted to explain how the Lost and Found attendant had "stolen" the camera.

"Maybe the lifeguard would have kept it for the owner," I told Sam.

"I don't think so," young Sam answered. "I saw the look in his eye, he would have kept it."

Sam learned something about human nature in these two encounters. He learned that people would lie to him and the best way to keep people honest was to have a system of accountability.

As we left the ranger's office Sam seemed to walk a little taller. He had done the adult thing. He found a lost item and tried to return it. So, if the owner didn't show up, he could keep it without a guilty conscience. No one came by our trailer that evening to claim the glove, nor did they write us in Chicago. Twenty-eight years later at the writing of this chapter, Sam still has the glove.

PRINCIPLES TO TAKE AWAY

1. The principle that people will lie to you. It seems little children naturally lie to people, they don't have to learn to lie, lying comes naturally from the heart. When the Bible says, "all men are liars," it meant mankind, for "all women are also liars." Ask a child if he took a cookie when you told him not to, and the child will shake his head no. Yet, that same child who will lie to you, will later in life be surprised when someone lies to them. Does that mean we should teach our children to be skeptical? No. So, what can we teach our children? First, teach them that they should expect people to tell them the truth. Therefore, our children should tell others the truth. Second, teach our children they should never be surprised when someone lies to them, especially if it's to the person's advantage. For money, pride or position, people might lie. Third, help people tell the truth by making them accountable to the truth. We would have given the glove to anyone who could describe it.

2. The principle of accountability. People tend to tell the truth when they know someone is checking up on them. Our children learned that people would claim a lost camera, but they couldn't identify it. So, it did not belong to them. We taught them that the real owners could identify their property, therefore we were accountable to return what we found to the owners. Finally, we taught the children they were responsible to try to return lost property. They had to try to find the owner, even leaving their name and address. And when the owner never claimed the baseball glove, Sam was allowed to keep it with a clear conscience.

3. The principle of living above other people. Ruth and I tried to teach our children not to live like other people, or to keep things without attempting to find the owners. My mother often told me "You're a Towns, I expect better of you." I communicated to my kids what my mother told me. Whereas many people will keep something they've found, I tried to teach my children to live higher than others, without acting snobby. Tell the truth when others don't.

A Christian should attempt to live above his/her lower nature in both word and deed. We should never take the lower road but take the higher road.

CHAPTER FIVE

CLASSIC COMICS: LEARNING RESPONSIBILITY

"How much can we spend on dinner?" Polly asked as we got out of the car and headed into the restaurant. It was a "Mom and Pop" type of diner in Winona Lake, Indiana, where we spent the summers of 1966, to 1970.

"First, let me see the prices on the menu," I told Polly.

"Let's go to McDonald's," Sam said. "We can get more food for our money!"

Because we were on a tight budget, the family only had a marginal amount to spend dining out. I taught at Winona Lake Summer School of Theology each summer where the pay was marginal. I got paid a week's salary for one month of teaching. But there were other benefits that made the job worthwhile. Pay included three meals a day in the school cafeteria, a meal for each of the five members of the Towns family.

Winona Lake was a Summer Bible Conference for where God's people could enjoy a vacation in a Christian environment. Some of the world's greatest Bible teachers had been coming each summer to Winona Lake for over 50 years. In association, a theological seminar had been established there. It was a great privilege for me and my family to enjoy the conferences. In return I taught four classes each day in the seminary.

Winona Lake had a number of activities for youth and children and the three Towns children took advantage of them all. But every once in a while, we wanted to go off the conference grounds for a meal, just to change our menu.

"How much can we spend?" Polly again asked as I was studying the menu. The average meal cost around one dollar and fifty cents in this restaurant in 1966, plus drink and dessert. So I told the kids,

"Two dollars and fifty cents a piece for dinner."

When the waitress seated us at a table, the kids immediately began studying the menu.

"I want a hamburger and two... not one... but two ice cream sundaes," was Sam's reply. "And a coke."

Polly was the sophisticated one of the three children. She ordered a meal an adult would like,

Veal cutlets" she said noting it cost one dollar and ninety-nine cents, so she had to decide between dessert or beverage. "I'll take water, and an apple pie," she said with the prissy attitude of a sophisticated teenager.

Debbie ordered her meal pointing out to me that it came at "Exactly two dollars and fifty cents... didn't I do good?"

On many occasions the family was taken to dinner after I spoke in a church. If my kids ordered the most expensive thing on the menu, there might be criticism of "the preacher's spoiled kids." I feel the same about me and my wife. We never order the most expensive on the menu, just as a Christian testimony.

The kids knew our family testimony was important. And beyond that, I was a gospel minister who was expected to hold a good testimony to Jesus Christ. Some people who took us to meals meant it when they said, "order anything on the menu." Others said, "order anything," but would be critical if we did.

So, the kids watched me when I looked over the menu when we were in a fancy restaurant. I'd hold up the number of fingers that represented the number of dollars they could spend. They'd just sit like little cherubs, watching me study the menu. Then my fingers went up—of course the host didn't see—to let Debbie, Sam and Polly know their limit. As soon as they had a dollar limit, they opened the menu to study prices and figure what was good. Winona Lake Conference center was a protected place where the kids could roam the whole city—without our fear that any harm would come to them. There were souvenir stores, all kinds of places to eat and a lot of summer fun things to do.

I didn't want the kids to always be asking for money for something to eat or begging for some type of toy. So, I gave them each a dollar every morning. They could buy what they wanted, but when it was gone... it was gone. I wanted to give them freedom yet teach them responsibility. I thought a dollar a day was excellent tuition for the lessons they would learn in managing their own life.

I usually gave out the dollars right before I went to my first class at 8:00 A.M. The difference in humans was reflected in the way my three kids spent their money.

Money burnt a hole in Debbie's pocket, and she went straight to the shops, as though she had to spend it before the morning was over. She'd go in a store, like a dime store, where she'd compare items, eliminating what she didn't want. She'd usually save just enough money for something special to eat or drink.

Sam was tight, he usually didn't even carry his money around in his pocket. He kept his money in his bedroom, usually in a jar or box. Sam always had money squirreled away.

Polly was unpredictable. She'd spend it all with Debbie one day, then save it all for two or three days... for a special prize.

One night, we found a unique store hidden on a back street of a neighboring town, Warsaw, Indiana. This little drug store had cluttered windows which were dusty. We walked in this cluttered little store out of boredom. We walked in because we had gone in every other store in town and didn't have anything else to do.

There in the back, almost hidden from customers' view we found a treasure, dozens of Classic Comics. These comic books were published in the 1960s with over 125 different titles of the greatest classic stories available to the English-speaking world. . . *Deerslayer* by James Fenimore Cooper, *David Copperfield* by William Dickins, plus *Tom Sawyer, Little Women, Two Years Before the Mast*, and many other magnificent treasures. Dozens of titles at $1.00 each.

I bought three comic books that first evening. It was *Deerslayer* for Sam, *Little Women* for Debbie, and I forget what comic book Polly got.

When we got back to our cabin, all three kids read a Classic Comic that evening. The next morning, they didn't go to the shops to play. They hung around the house reading each other's Classic Comics.

That evening we returned to the dingy shop, went to the back aisle and sorted through the available titles. Choosing *Gulliver's Travels*, I bought only one book that evening, at one dollar per book, I was not financially prepared to buy one for each of them.

"Loan me a dollar. . ." Sam asked me for money. Then he promised,

"I'll pay you when I get back to the cabin." He was stingy with his money, but he wanted to buy one even though I promised to buy another Classic Comic each day we came to Warsaw. Sam was willing to part with his money for a Classic Comic. He got *A Knight in King Arthur's Court.*

"He... he... he...," the owner laughed when I went to pay for the two books that night.

"Saw ya' here last night... you're back for more," he boasted. We didn't say much the first night when I bought the first books.

Classic Comics: Learning Responsibility

"How come you sell classic comics?" I asked the odd-looking store owner. I had never seen Classic Comics for sale in any other store. As a small kid I subscribed for one year. So, I knew about the great dreams they could teach a child.

"My children read them ...," the owner explained how much the comic books had helped his kids. So, he ordered a large supply for parents to buy for their kids. There were a large number of lake cabins in that part of Indiana. He knew the parents from the Midwest spent time in the region each summer. He thought parents would be as motivated as he was to purchase Classic Comics. But he was mistaken. Parents didn't come to his store. Parents didn't buy Classic Comics. His merchandise just sat on the shelves.

"Modern kids want modern comic books ...," the store owner complained. His sad voice described modern kids who just watched television and read the action comics.

"Comics without a message," he criticized them.

"I'll be back," explaining my kids would just read all three books all in a day or two. "They will love Classic Comics," I boasted.

"Will you save them for me?" I asked.

"Don't worry....," he assured me. "These Classics have been here for three or four years," he complained. "Other parents won't buy them out in a month."

We went back almost every night to get another Classic Comic, *Three Musketeers*, or *Moby Dick*, or *The Tale of Two Cities*. In addition to the dollar allowances I'd give the kids each morning, I'd pay the dollar to buy them a Classic Comic in the evening. Sometimes I'd just park at the curb and hand them a dollar. The three kids ran in to the store to get their reading adventure for the next day.

On many evenings, Sam took his dollar to make sure he got his choice for his next day's reading. Like most boys, he wanted adventure, action or stories about boys, like *Tom Sawyer* or *Huck Finn*.

This project of buying, reading, and saving Classic Comics went on for three summers at Winona Lake, Indiana. When our family bought every title from the dingy little store, I mailed an order to the publisher to buy all the titles we didn't have. Even back then, the publishers didn't have all of their back copies in print. There were four or five titles that we never got. Eventually, Sam has about 120 copies of Classic Comics in his possession. He says they are his. The girls say some belong to them. But possession is 9/10 of the law and Sam has them. Remember, Sam is the saver.

PRINCIPLES TO TAKE AWAY

1. The principle that "money is life." I believe money is more than a symbol of barter, a symbol of wealth or a symbol of success. Money is life. We give our time and energy to our work, and in return get money. So, money is a symbolic representation of life. The money in our pocket represents tangibly our life. Debbie was the child of my youth; she came through our most difficult financial days. So, when she got some money, she exchanged it for immediate gratification. She wanted to have all the things she never had. Sam was the saver. He reacted differently to poverty. He saved his money because he might not get any more.

2. The principle of developing character by choice. I knew the kids would squander a lot of the money I gave them in daily allowances, but to me it was tuition. I felt they would learn many lessons in life, whether they wasted money or whether they made good choices. First, I didn't want them running to me or Ruth every time they had a whim or every time they wanted something. One of the greatest lessons Debbie learned was when she bought a toy early in the morning, the toy was soon broken, and she had nothing to eat or drink for the rest of the day.

"I didn't really need the toy," she told me that evening.

Second, the kids learned to make choices. I didn't have to say "Yes" or "No," or "It's too much." I let them make decisions. Learning to spend money is one of the early ways that our children learned to make good and bad choices. A daily allowance was helping them become an autonomous individual.

3. <u>The principle of learning through consequences</u>. I believe we live in a world where people are separated from their consequences. Welfare payments to help the poor are needed, but not the kind of welfare that destroys human initiative. Good welfare helps a person through a problem, but our welfare reinforces mistakes, i.e. a single mother on welfare is rewarded for having more babies. People make bad choices because they are lazy, or they drop out of school and are not qualified for a job. Yet, that person never suffers the consequence of their bad choices. The safety net we call welfare hurts human incentive.

I wanted my kids to feel the consequences of bad choice, such as spending too early, buying the wrong thing, or not buying at all. Children need to learn from consequences, but not the type of consequences that will hurt them for a lifetime. They need a protected environment where they could make mistakes yet learn from them without suffering for all their life.

4. <u>The principle of harmonizing freedom and accountability</u>. When we went in a restaurant, the kids had the freedom to choose what they wanted to eat, but there were limits, i.e. financial limits. Some define freedom as allowing a child to do what they want to do. But biblical freedom is allowing the child to choose what is best. My wife and I tried to develop discipline in our children by the way we allowed them to spend money. We were hoping bad decisions would be stepping-stones to future self-control.

5. <u>The principle of remembering children are children</u>. Most children want immediate gratification. Children want what makes them happy and they want it NOW. But maturity has learned to postpone gratification. To children it is "play now and pay later."

So, I bought my children Classic Comics after they spent all their money on something else. I didn't want to reward them (buy comics), I wanted them to feel the consequences of poor decisions. But I also wanted them to develop an appetite for reading great books. So, I remembered that children are children, and we should always do what is best for the child. I started buying Classic Comics for them. Then Sam bought some Classic Comics. Finally, Debbie and Polly bought some. Also, even though each girl spent her dollar during the day and Sam saved his dollar back in the cabin, we all usually stopped for some ice cream or other snack each evening, and I bought.

CHAPTER SIX

MONOPOLY: WHEN LOSING IS WINNING

"Let's beat Dad," Debbie boasted to Sam and Polly. We were all stretched out on the living room floor playing Monopoly.

"Trade me Boardwalk," Debbie snickered to Sam. Then she laughed putting her hand to her mouth, "I'll give you the Electric Company for your Boardwalk." Debbie was proposing that Sam give her the most valuable piece of property in Monopoly for one of the cheapest. Since trading was legal, what Debbie was doing was legal, but I didn't think so. She was not playing to win; she was playing to beat me.

"Hey...!!!" I yelled out in anguish. "That's not fair."

Debbie and Polly snickered, Sam got that boyish grin that only a pre-teen can flash when he wants to do something devilish, when he wants to challenge the authority in the family, i.e. the father. Debbie added, "I'll trade you New York when Dad gets to the other side of the board," she was figuring out ways to bankrupt me in Monopoly. She told Sam, "When you have New York, build a hotel and charge Dad a lot more money."

"Hey...!!!" I again cried out in anguish. "You kids are ganging up on me."

When the kids were small, I wanted to give them a passion for winning. I didn't want my kids to be like hippies. I thought hippies were people who just sit around with no ambition, no competitive nature, no purpose in life. I figured if I could develop a strong competitive edge, my kids would make something of their life. So, Monopoly was one tool that I used to teach my kids to play, so they could compete in the game of life.

On Saturday mornings when I didn't have classes, we set up the Monopoly game on the living room floor. Also, it kept them from too much cartoon viewing and provided me quality time with the kids. Not only on Saturdays, we played Monopoly during vacations and holidays.

When it came to playing Monopoly with the kids, I could have taken one of two strategies. I could have been a loving father who allowed his kids to win. But I was afraid that would make them passive. When a little kid beats his father in Monopoly, and the kid knows that his father knows Monopoly better than he does, he does not really learn a sense of winning by beating Dad. Even little children know when they have been coddled by their parents.

The other strategy was to play them hard and beat them. I figured when I beat my kids honestly, that would put a fire in their belly to reciprocate, i.e. to beat me.

A few times I tried the "coddling" approach. I let my children win. But that didn't seem to satisfy them, nor did it satisfy me. When they won, they would run into the kitchen to tell Mom, and even the way that Ruth responded told them that Dad had let them win. So, when I played Monopoly with the kids, I played to win.

Eventually, the kids became competitive with one another. Polly the youngest usually got beat, but she always played because she wanted to be included in whatever was going on. It was Debbie and Sam who developed a cutthroat spirit to win. Debbie was only one year older than Sam. So, he had to use his cunning wit to make up for that one year of experience that Debbie had on him. Polly watched while Debbie and Sam tried to beat each other. To this day, Polly doesn't like Monopoly, and now that she's older she won't play with the family.

But when it came to playing Dad in Monopoly, all three kids banded together to beat me. Debbie and Sam usually fussed a lot, about a lot of things, but not about Monopoly. They became best friends when they played and beat me. They sacrificed their money, their property; they even sacrificed personal winning, if the other could beat Dad.

Being a legalist, I insisted the kids following the rules as far as mortgaging property to the bank, trading property with one another, or any other transaction. Debbie and Sam followed the rules, but they suppressed personal desires and animosity to beat me. So, Debbie traded Sam Boardwalk just because I was ready to roll the dice with the prospect of passing Boardwalk AND Park Place. Sam quickly mortgaged other property to put hotels on both properties in order to bankrupt me. When I got to the other side of the board, Sam traded Debbie New York so Debbie could build houses or hotels to catch me.

Who usually won?

When we first started playing Monopoly, I used to win all of the time, I was older, wiser and after all I was the dad. But it didn't take the kids very long to become traders. They started giving up their prized property, just so the other could beat me. Before long I was systematically being defeated by either Debbie, Sam, and on occasions they gave their property to Polly, and even the youngest of the three beat me soundly.

Who won?

I won... I won even when I lost.

There was no way I could lose.

Obviously, when I won Monopoly, I was winner. When I lost at

Monopoly, I got what I wanted. I was teaching my children to be competitive; I was giving them a spirit of competition. And my kids were learning to handle money which is learning how to handle life. They were learning how to make change, how to negotiate a deal, and how to buy and sell property.

Obviously, many of other children have learned to play Monopoly and have developed a competitive spirit, but my kids developed a winning spirit.

Like most games that children play, after a while they get tired of Monopoly and moved on to other interests. Monopoly no longer held the alluring mystery that it once had. Since there was no challenge, the kids moved on to chess, and other board games. Then one day at the lake, while vacationing at someone's lake cottage in Canada, Sam and Debbie decided to join their Monopoly board with the Monopoly board they found at the cottage. They combined the money, and created a game called DOUBLE MONOPOLY, which took twice as long to play. They could buy twice as much property and gain twice as much money. One person could own two Park Places and two Boardwalks. They played one game of DOUBLE MONOPOLY for two weeks.

Again, I was the winner. I had taught my children to be creative and challenged them to be competitive. I didn't create DOUBLE MONOPOLY, so I was not as wise as the kids. They beat me every time. So, I refused to play. Finally, Debbie said,

"Come on and play DOUBLE MONOPOLY with us Dad," she pleaded. "We won't gang up on you," she promised. "We'll all play by ourselves; we'll all play to win."

So, I played DOUBLE MONOPOLY with the kids two or three times. But they had started playing DOUBLE MONOPOLY before I had, so they knew the tricks of the trade. They knew how to get ahead and what worked best. I never won at DOUBLE MONOPOLY, even when I played my best and they played for themselves... without helping one another.

Monopoly: When Losing is Winning

Once a minister visited our house and played Monopoly with the kids. Quickly into the game the kids got disgusted with him. He landed on a very valuable piece of property, I think it was Pennsylvania, but he didn't buy it. He just threw the dice and moved on.

"That's not the way to play...," Debbie observed.

It happened a second time.

"Why don't you buy it," Sam asked.

"I don't want it."

My kids realized he was just goofing off. Sam complained that the minister wasn't really playing by the spirit of the game, he wasn't trying to win.

A little later into the game, when the minister needed money, he just reached over to take some of Polly's money.

"I am just borrowing it."

"No," Polly said.

"But I need it." And he went on playing.

The visiting minister didn't play by the spirit of the game, nor by the rules of the game. He was just entertaining the kids... trying to be funny. When the dice rolled a number he didn't want, he would sweep them away and roll again until he got the number he wanted.

"We don't want to play with him anymore," Debbie said after he left. She explained in her childish way, "it's no fun winning if he doesn't try." Then she added, "it's no fun losing when he cheats... it's just no fun at all."

PRINCIPLES TO TAKE AWAY

1. The principle of competitiveness. Competition is a natural force of life, and children who learn to handle competition usually get

ahead. Children have to learn to win and win by the rules; and they have to learn to lose, for we don't always win in life.

Since there are no free lunches in life, guaranteed winning lottery tickets, or pots of gold at the end of the rainbow, I felt it was important to develop a competitive spirit in my kids so they would make their own way. I choose Monopoly as a tool to develop a winning spirit, and I probably did the job too well.

After my children married, one spouse noted the competitiveness of my children and said, "Why do all of you Towns have to win?" Then added, "you need to learn to be happy when you lose."

A few days later we were playing Rook, men against the women, and this spouse was beaten badly, so badly that it showed in facial displeasure. "Are you happy losing," I said.

That became a defining moment for that spouse and from that moment on, determined to be a winner.

2. <u>The principle that play prepared for life</u>. My kids sharpened their ability to handle money by playing Monopoly. Once when we were checking out of McDonald's, I had given the clerk a ten-dollar bill to pay for our order. She messed up the calculation and gave me too little change. She recalculated and gave me too much change. The embarrassing thing was that she was older than all three of my kids, yet as they stood there, they had immediately picked up how much change I was owed.

"She didn't play Monopoly when she was little...," Polly said.

3. <u>The principle of finding happiness within rules</u>. Sometimes kids fuss about the rules around the house, what time to be home, cleaning their room, and other such rules. But when it comes to Monopoly, kids learn that they are happier when everyone plays by the rules. When someone "goofed off" with the money or the dice, it killed the incentive for the others to win. So when everyone plays by the rules, the game is much more enjoyable, and competition is more meaningful. Then the

winner feels better because he has kept the rules, and the looser feels the regret of losing, even though they played within the rules.

CHAPTER SEVEN

THE PHOTO CONTEST:
TEACHING CREATIVITY

"Do we hafta?" the kids complained from the backseat of our Chevy Impala. They were buried in comic books and didn't want to get out of the car to go sightseeing. We were on the top of a mountain and I was trying to motivate my kids to get out of the car to see the fantastic views.

"You can see five states from up there," I pointed to a rock point. I wanted them to climb to the top of the peak where the lookout tower was located. The advertisement claimed, "See five states."

We were on the top of Rock City, Tennessee, just outside of Chattanooga. It was our summer vacation, and usually we left greater Chicago, Illinois, to visit my boyhood home in Savannah, Georgia. Halfway between Chicago and Savannah was Rock City, on the top of Lookout Mountain. I had never seen five states from one location, and I thought it was important to see all five at one time. Also, I thought it was important for my kids to see all five states from Rock City.

"Do we hafta?" Debbie was the spokesperson.

"You can read comics any time," I argued.

"We wanta read now..." Debbie let the words trail off.

"You'll miss seeing five states," I said.

"That's O.K."

"No," I said, "it's not okay." I was irritated because I wanted the kids to be as interested in seeing the things I wanted to see.

I made the kids put down their comics and I made them climb to the observation tower to see five states.

They sulked.

I was irritated.

No one was happy.

But we all saw five states from Rock City.

The following summer we planned a vacation from Chicago to Winnipeg, then across Canada down the Pacific Coast to Los Angeles and Disneyland. On this trip we'd see the Canadian Rockies and the breath-taking scenery of the Northwest. We'd see the Golden Gate Bridge and the giant Redwoods of the Sequoia Forest. We'd see the Grand Canyon, the Painted Desert, the Mile-High Bridge and many other wonders of nature. Our trip to the West coast was a "once-in-a-lifetime" trip that would take a month.

"How can I get the kids to look and learn?" I asked myself. I didn't want to fight with them every time we came to an observation tower or scenic overlook. One day I came up with the idea of a photography contest. I announced to the kids:

"You can win ninety dollars on this trip for taking great pictures."

The kids were only mildly motivated. They were not interested in taking pictures; they were interested in ninety dollars. That was more money than they ever had in their life. But they were still not gung-ho about a photography contest.

Why?

Because I was taking a photography course because of a position I had as Sunday School Editor of *Christian Life* magazine. I was full-time professor at Trinity Evangelical Divinity School, and writing articles about churches provided research for my ministry. I took the course to learn how to take pictures for the magazine. I found it was twice as easy to sell an article if I had pictures of the stories I wrote. While taking the course, I tried to get my kids to pose for pictures and they didn't like being Dad's guinea pig. So, at first they didn't warm up to the idea of the photography contest.

I didn't want them to take pictures because I was interested in photography. I wanted them to take pictures to develop their power of observation. If they were looking for better pictures to take, they would see the memorable sights on our vacation.

"Fifteen Dollars for first prize in each category," I explained. Each one could win at least fifteen dollars and that was more than they had ever had. There were three categories:

* Point of interest or landscape.

* Human interest: a picture of someone that was unique.

* Humor: something funny.

The ninety dollars was split into three prizes; fifteen dollars for first place; ten dollars for second place; and five dollars for third place.

The kids had to use my camera because we didn't have money to buy each of them a camera. We wrote down the number on the film for each picture. I sometimes helped them with the f-stop or the timing of the shutter. They had to take the actual shot, or if they wanted to be in the picture, they had to line up the camera for me or Ruth to shoot the picture. The day finally came when we took off for Canada. Within the first hour we faced a life-defining problem. What the kids thought was a point of interest was not always what I thought was a point of interest. I didn't want to stop where they wanted to stop. When we crossed from Illinois into Wisconsin, the first test came.

"Stop the car," Sam yelled. "Go back," he barked.

Sam saw a man pull a fish from a lake in Wisconsin. Sam had to take that picture. Sam liked fishing, but I didn't care for fishing. Much as I didn't want to, I stopped the car, turned around and returned to a small fishing camp. We got out of the car and walked out on the short rickety dock.

"Can I take a picture of your fish?" Sam asked.

"Why?"

When I explained about the photography contest the fisherman pulled two small fishes out of the water, hooked to a chain. They were particularly small. He held them up and Sam took the picture.

"Thanks."

We were on our way. It was an interesting picture but later didn't win any prize. When we got it developed, the perspective made the fish so small, no one could see them at first glance.

We had to make a rule about stopping to take pictures. We decided that everyone had to agree before we'd stop the car. Otherwise, we'd get behind on our schedule. We had planned to stay with friends in each major city on our journey. So, if we didn't arrive on the scheduled date, everything was messed up. Also, I was to preach in their churches in exchange for bed and breakfast. So, I had to be in certain places on time. We were crossing the Canadian prairies when Polly pointed out the front windshield to a patch of sparkling yellow on the horizon.

"Look at that yellow field."

"Those are sunflowers," I explained. "People raise sunflowers for a living."

"To sell flowers?" Debbie asked.

"No," I shook my head negatively. "People eat sunflower seeds."

"Air Snakes," Debbie yelled.

"Air Snake... Air Snake... Air Snake," all the kids chanted.

The Photo Contest: Teaching Creativity

"Honest," I pleaded for them to believe me. But they had never heard of people eating sunflower seeds, so they doubted me.

We pulled off the road to take some pictures of the yellow fields. But when we got close, the yellow blanket we saw in the distance wasn't solid yellow. Up close we saw a lot of dirt between each flower stalk.

"We won't get our yellow picture," I commented to the kids.

Sam was the jokester, so he handed me his camera and instructed,

"Take a picture of me when I yell..."

Sam walked out into the yellow field of sunflowers. They must have been a hybrid, for the yellow sunflowers were waist height, not head high that I remembered sunflowers back in Georgia. He pulled a yellow sunflower up by the roots... flower, stem and a glob of dirt. Then holding the one prized yellow sunflower above his head, he yelled.

"Shoot!"

I aimed and clicked.

That picture earned Sam a first prize in humor and fifteen dollars. The fact he was grinning a "Jack Horner" grin helped to win the prize. The picture not only had a beautiful background of yellow, it centered on one flower, root and dirt lifted triumphantly to the sky. Sam was like Jack Horner who stuck his thumb into the pie, and pulled out a plum and said, "What a good boy am I."

A little later Debbie won her first prize in the Canadian Rockies for a picture of the corkscrew tunnel. We had read about this unique tunnel where you could see a train going into a tunnel and coming out the exit. The train tracks coming down a valley was so steep that the brakes on the train would heat up, wear out, and a runaway train would inevitably have a wreck. Engineers dug a circular tunnel into the side of the mountain to take the steep descent out of the grade. What made their tunnel famous was that you could see the front of a train coming out the tunnel a few hundred feet below the end of the train going into the tunnel.

We stopped at a picnic area about ten miles from the tunnel. Not that many trains came through that place in the Canadian Rockies. I wanted to see that tunnel with two entrances. I wanted to see a train go in and come out of the tunnel at the same time.

"Too bad we can't see a train in the tunnel," I said to the kids.

Ruth was fixing lunch. We had bought a loaf of bread, bologna and mayonnaise. There were no hamburger stands in that part of the Rockies, so we were fixing sandwiches. We were sitting at a picnic table next to the train tracks. The sandwiches were half made when Debbie heard a train coming.

"Hurry," she announced. "I want a picture of a train in Corkscrew Tunnel."

Everyone instantly jumped into action. The bread, bologna and mayonnaise were swept up in one motion into a paper bag. Everyone ran for the car. I hit the acceleration and we threw rocks as we roared off to the Corkscrew Tunnel.

"This will be a picture of a lifetime," Debbie hung over the front set talking to me about the settings on the camera. "Hurry up," she pushed me. "I'll get my camera ready."

The sign pointed left to a scenic overview of Corkscrew Tunnel.

"The train's not here yet," Debbie told us what we all could see.

"This is my picture," Debbie announced, "I called it first." We all agreed.

As we were waiting for the train to enter the tunnel, I told the kids how fortunate we were to get there at the exact time.

"We will see what very few people actually see."

"And we'll have a picture," Debbie added.

The Photo Contest: Teaching Creativity

Then I began to think out loud. This was a great coincidence, but there was another that would be too much to expect.

"Wouldn't it be great to see an aircraft carrier go under the Golden Gate Bridge in San Francisco?" I innocently asked out loud.

"I claim it..." Polly was the first to speak, "It's my picture," she demanded.

Debbie got her unique picture of the same train going in and coming out of the same tunnel at the same time. She won first prize for Point of Interest and landscape, and fifteen dollars.

A week later we were in San Francisco touring the city. We had spent the morning riding the cable cars, seeing Chinatown, and losing our hearts in the city by the bay. At about two o'clock in the afternoon, we were on the top of Spyglass Hill, sitting on the grass, looking at the navy yards. There was one aircraft carrier at the dock.

Wouldn't it be nice to see it leave?" I asked. "We could see it go under the Golden Gate Bridge."

"And I could get my picture," Polly added.

"Dad," Sam saw it first. "Look at the sailors; they're throwing the ropes on to the dock." Then Sam continued to tell what he saw, "I think it is getting ready to leave."

I saw the tugboats begin to pull feverishly on the aircraft carrier. I realized it was moving from the dock.

"Run for the car," I commanded. Debbie and Polly get to the Chevy first. I frantically picked up the blanket, junk and the camera. I brought up the rear. I didn't know the way to the Golden Gate Bridge, so I just headed West. I was fearful I'd get stuck in traffic in a strange city and miss the aircraft carrier going under the bridge. I was picking my way through traffic trying to find a way to the Golden Gate Bridge.

"Watch for signs," I told Ruth, "There should be a sign to point to the bridge."

"Get your camera ready," I told Polly. Then I told Sam and Debbie,

"Let Polly sit next to the window so she can shoot a picture of the aircraft carrier."

As we approached the entrance to the Golden Gate Bridge, the aircraft carrier was a few hundred yards away heading straight for us. I wanted to slow down so Polly could shoot straight down on the carrier's deck. But the highway over the Golden Gate Bridge is an expressway. You can't slow down. You can't stop. I slowed down as much as I could, and Polly got her shot. It was a first-place winner of the unique photograph. While it was not as clearly focused as the others, technically it was blurred because we were moving. But she won the unique perspective category and fifteen dollars.

The photography contest was one of the better ideas we tried to get the kids to properly experience the world around them. The kids got their money, each won thirty dollars. I got them to look carefully at the once in a lifetime sights they were seeing. And we both learned; they learned about their country and I learned how to motivate children.

PRINCIPLES TO TAKE AWAY

1. <u>The principle of motivating by self-interest</u>. Parents learn early that their kids are not always interested in the things that parents are interested in. But when we appeal to their self-interest, we can motivate their interest. My kids wanted money, and I wanted them to learn on our vacation, so a photography contest to earn money helped accomplish that goal.

In a small world that's only filled with their selfish concerns. Some children read comic books and let the greatest experience of life pass them by. The child who has the most rewarding experience has the richest life, not the child with the most money. Parents should not let their kids pull a bucket over their heads to keep from becoming involved in life's experiences. But parents can't make their children do what they don't want to do. It's usually counter-productive. Parents must motivate their children to experience the good things of life and to experience things that will broaden their world. Parents can't let children squander their future on the tyranny of present desires.

2. The principle of creating creativity. We can't teach our children to be creative from a textbook. They learn creativity by being creative. I wanted to get my kids to pay attention to the things I thought were important, and I thought a photo contest would keep us from arguing on our vacation. I did get these benefits, but also there was something greater. The kids learned creativity by trying to take better pictures to win first prize. They began to think up special ways to shoot pictures and special arrangement of people in their pictures. It was great, the kids were learning, and I was happy.

3. The principle of future creativity. Not only did my photo contest teach the kids creativity and to pay attention, they began to stake out future turf. Debbie planned her picture at the Corkscrew Tunnel long before we got there. Polly planned to take a picture of an aircraft carrier sailing under the Golden Gate Bridge a week before we got there. When they were planning for the future, and valuing the future, they were forming adult perspectives of life.

CHAPTER EIGHT

AWANA: MAKE ME LEARN

"Make me learn this," Sam stood before my desk in my office at home, pushing his AWANA books toward me. "I can't learn the verses before AWANA," he was desperate.

It was 5:00 p.m. wintertime. The winter in Chicago was dark and the sun had disappeared an hour ago. Because it was black outside, Sam thought it was time to go to AWANA, and he did not know his verses.

"Make me learn these verses...," he repeated himself.

Sam already had on his AWANA shirt, a gray long sleeve shirt with epaulets on the shoulders. Ruth had sewed the patches at the appropriate places on the shirt and when he memorized enough verses, he won another star on his ribbons. The ribbons looked like the kind soldiers were awarded. Sam pinned these ribbons over his pocket. And for faithful attendance at Sunday school, Sam won hash marks to be worn on the sleeve. Ruth sewed them on as soon as he won another.

"I'll get another star...," he paused, "if I can say these verses without a mistake."

"H-m-m-m-m," I thought. "This is a victory," I kept my thoughts to myself. I remember the nights I almost begged Sam to memorize his verses. Now, he was begging me for help. This was one of those life-changing moments.

I had wanted Sam to join Boy Scouts, just as I had joined the Scouts when I turned 12 years old. As he came of age we lived in Canada, and the Canadians didn't have Cub Scouts (the organization for boys not yet 12 years old). They called it the Wolf Pack in Canada. Sam joined the Wolf Pack and got started at Bethesda Church in Winnipeg. It was a character-building organization with Christian principles, but it included more that just Christians. The Boy Scouts and the Wolf Pack gave boys outdoor skills like hiking, tying knots and cooking over an open fire. Sam went to the "overnights" with the Wolf Pack in Canada.

When we moved to greater Chicago so I could teach in Trinity Evangelical Divinity School, we joined North Suburban Evangelical Free Church. It was a great family church but didn't have Cub Scouts or Boy Scouts. I began looking around for a Scout troop for Sam. When I asked my pastor about Boy Scouts, he sent John Hoefling to talk with me about Awana.

"Let me tell you about AWANA," John said when he came to my home to see me.

"Let's get Sam to hear this...," I recommended. So, I called my son into the living room where John Hoefling and I were talking. Sam took a seat across the room and just listened. He didn't get involved in the conversation.

"AWANA is a Christian club," John began his explanation. He was the leader of AWANA at North Suburban Evangelical Free Church. "The boys wear uniforms." John had a catalog that showed the gray shirt, but there were no scout pants. The boys wore their blue jeans. It didn't seem as snappy as the Boy Scout uniform had with leggings, shirt and hat. Blue jeans didn't seem sophisticated to me.

"The boys win patches, hash marks for attending Sunday school, and they get ribbons for memorizing Scriptures." John explained the benefit of getting the Word of God into children. I didn't need to be convinced, because I knew the benefit in my life of memorizing the Bible.

Something was wrong... not wrong in the sense of leading my boy astray. Something was missing with AWANA. I thumbed through the AWANA catalog and it was not the same as Boy Scouts. As I listened to John Hoefling, he wasn't describing a club like Boy Scouts. I again flipped through the pages of the catalog. I was looking for something that was missing.

"Where's the knot tying?" I asked. Then I added with some displeasure, "What about camping out and cooking meals over an open fire?"

"We don't do that...," John didn't even answer my objections. He ignored my questions.

"AWANA builds Christian character," John explained. "Your boy will memorize the Bible... he will grow in Christ... he will have Christian friends."

John explained the games the boys played at AWANA and competition in the AWANA circle. He described the AWANA Olympics where boys from one church played AWANA members from other churches. Each spring a giant AWANA Olympics motivated the boys to develop a winning spirit through competition.

"But memorizing Bible verses every week will change Sam's life," was John Hoefling's hammering point.

After he emphasized the Christian objective of AWANA, John answered my objections about the outdoors program of the church. John explained the church was involved in Camp Willowby just up in Wisconsin over the Illinois border. Not only did Camp Willowby provide a Christian camp experience, the boys would take canoe wilderness trips where they pitched tents, cooked over an open flame and paddled from lake to lake.

"Please," Sam finally broke into the conversation, "Let me join AWANA... Tim goes each week." I didn't know it but Sam was already convinced he wanted to join AWANA. Since Sam's best friend went to AWANA, I relented. It was one of the best decisions I've ever made for Sam. AWANA gave my son a strong biblical basis to develop character.

The letters in AWANA are an acrostic from the verse, "Approved Workers Are Not Ashamed." While AWANA had both boys' and girls' programs, our church only had boys AWANA.

When Sam first began AWANA, he didn't memorize his verses for several weeks. He didn't do it by himself and I didn't know what had happened. I knew Sam liked the program and looked forward to going every Friday night. What I didn't know was that Sam was falling behind the rest of his friends. Each time a boy memorized a page or verse, his instructor signed the page, and when enough pages were completed, the boys got a ribbon to wear on their chest, just like a soldier in the army. Next, with more verses, they won stars to go on their ribbons. Sam's friend was getting ahead in patches and ribbons. Finally, one day after church, John Hoefling stopped me after the church service.

"Sam's not keeping up..." I was embarrassed when John told me the other boys were doing better.

"Can you help Sam memorize his verses?" John asked.

"Sure."

I didn't know I was supposed to help him memorize his verses.

"I help Tim every week just before we go to AWANA," John explained. "That way, the boys can recite them perfectly when they first get there."

The following week Sam and I went over the verses. He knew every verse perfectly and the instructor signed his book. For the next few weeks Sam aced his verses, and got his book signed. When he brought his first ribbon home, Ruth and I were proud. We all felt like we grew a little; we all felt like we climbed another rung on the ladder called, "growing up."

For about a year, every Friday night Ruth and I would get the book, make Sam sit down, and make him learn his verses. We took the initiative, but he followed willingly. We always had to remind him about his verses, but he was the one who did the actual memorizing.

Then came that eventful winter night when Sam passed from childhood to young manhood. He took responsibility for his verse. He brought his book into my office at home and asked,

"Help me learn these verses..."

Then handing me the AWANA book, Sam sat in the chair beside my desk. We began repeating the verses he needed to know that evening,

I listened... he repeated.

I corrected... he repeated.

I nodded approval... he repeated.

After that night, I still helped Sam with his verses, but it was different. I no longer had to take the initiative, memorizing the verse became his responsibility. He brought the book to me and I listened to him as he repeated verse after verse... page after page.

Sam won ribbon after ribbon... trophy after trophy and eventually won the highest award that AWANA at North Suburban Evangelical Free Church offered. Sam won the Timothy Award. Today the Timothy Award is just the beginning of the highest awards that AWANA offers. Today they have the Meritous Award and other achievements. But in the 1960s in Northern Chicago, Illinois, Sam won the highest award offered by Awana. And the Bible he memorized has been a foundation for his ministry for Christ.

PRINCIPLES TO TAKE AWAY

1. <u>The principle of substitute dreams</u>. Even though many parents try, they can't live their dreams in the lives of their children. Most parents have good dreams for their children, and most parents want their children to experience the good things they had when they were children. But children have different temperaments than their parents, they have different I.Q.s, different environmental pressures, different friends, different spiritual gifts, and God probably has a different plan for their life. And confess it, your parents used different methods in raising you, which means your kids will be raised differently than you. So, don't try to make them live out your dreams. Even if Boy Scouts was great for you, AWANA may be better for your kids.

2. <u>The principle of emotional support</u>. Our kids do better when they have the support of parents. Like memorizing verses, kids usually only give marginal effort, even when they are motivated with awards like ribbons and stars for successfully saying a page of verses. We have to hold their physical hands when they are small, and we hold their emotional hands as they transition into adulthood. The consequences were too great for not memorizing weekly verses, so I took the initiative. I prodded and Sam responded. But there came a day when it paid off. He took the initiative.

3. <u>The principle of transferred initiative</u>. Because children are children, they usually respond emotionally and have little self-discipline. Because children are children, they seek immediate gratification, they don't have the big picture, nor can they make decisions based on long-range goals. That is why God gave parents to children, because parents will think for their children and make decisions for their children. Parents have to be their children's standard. Parents have to take the initiative. Because children are children, they don't have it within themselves to make hard decisions or to discipline themselves... but after years of parental decision-making, guidance and support, there comes a day when the child begins to take the initiative for himself. That day won't come suddenly, nor will it come fully in one day. But slowly the child will begin to be responsible, then he will probably say something like, "Make me memorize these verses."

CHAPTER NINE

HORSESHOES: YOU CAN DO IT

Sam picked up the horseshoe and spit on the end. Spitting was his good luck symbol when he needed a ringer... and Sam desperately needed a ringer. From the other end of the horseshoe courts he heard the Scandinavian accent of the wee little man yelling,

"Sam, you're my man," encouraging words from Dr. Kenneth Scott Latourette the foremost church historian in all the world, some think of all time. Dr. Latourette wrote one of the most detailed and largest history of Christianity.

Dr. Latourette and my son were teammates in horseshoes at Winona Lake Campground, Winona Lake, Indiana. Their opponents were Dr. Donald Guthrie, the outstanding New Testament scholar from London University, England and Orlando Constas, a student of mine at the school and city-wide evangelist in South America.

"Come on Sam," Latourette excitedly yelled in his subdued Scandinavian accent, "You can make a ringer..."

Sam placed his right foot against the metal post and peered to the opposing steel post that seemed miles away. Sam was impervious to the greatness of intellect or academic reputation playing horseshoes with him.

Sam's partner was Dr. Kenneth Scott Latourette, a man who had written an eight-volume history of Christian missions and a five-volume history of the Christian church. Dr. Latourette probably knew more church history than any other man in the history of Christianity. Yet this world class scholar stopped by our dinner table, not to speak to me, a colleague and fellow teacher. Latourette asked to speak to Sam.

"I need you as my partner tonight," Latourette said to twelve-year-old Sam. "I can't win without you."

That night Sam would pitch horseshoes against Dr. Donald Guthrie of London, England, the famous author of scholarly works. Guthrie had flown from London University in England to teach at this small Midwest summer theological seminary in heartland U.S.A.

Dr. Guthrie had just thrown a ringer that won the game, now Sam had to top it. If Sam could top Guthrie's ringer with a ringer of his own, he and Latourette would win. They had eighteen points, and a ringer would give them a win. In those days they played that a ringer canceled the opponent and awarded five points.

"I can make a ringer if you pray ..." Sam yelled down the court to his partner Dr. Latourette. Sam's informality with such a great man bothered me. Growing up I had been intimidated by anyone who was influential, like the local pastor, the manager of the local grocery store, and the editor of the Savannah Evening Press where I was a paper carrier. But Sam talked with Dr. Latourette as if he was the man next door. He was as friendly with Dr. Latourette as he was with his grandpa.

Stepping away from the metal post, Sam went through a small routine that was supposed to give him confidence. Like a batter taking several practice swings before going to the plate, Sam took several practice pitches without releasing a horseshoe. Spitting on the end of the horseshoe, he placed his right heel against the pole. He was ready. The horseshoe court was quiet. Squinting his right eye, Sam swung the horseshoe taking a step forward, the horseshoe flew with centripetal force, completed a perfect arc, flipping once and clanging noisily against the pole; he scored a ringer.

Horseshoes: You Can Do It

"YEAH!" Latourette, lifted both fists into the sky. The wee little man triumphantly trotted toward Sam.

Sam dropped to one knee like a quarterback just throwing a touchdown. He bowed his head in gratitude.

Latourette slapped Sam on the back and did a little Irish jig. Victory was sweet. Beating Don Guthrie and Orlando Constas was the perfect touch to the evening.

The red sky stretched out over Winona Lake. The late summer sun gave its unique benediction. Crickets joined in evening symphony. The beauty of nature was made sweeter by the social interaction of a 12-year-old boy and a wee little man from Europe that had accomplished the goal of the day—they won at horseshoes. The grandeur of life is determined by such small events as friendly competition among friends.

Winona Lake campgrounds had attracted the elite leaders of American Christianity. The world-famous evangelist Billy Sunday had his home there, had built a revival tabernacle seating 10,000 people and the choir loft could seat another 2,500. The choir loft was much larger than most American churches. Because the greatest speakers came from all over America to the campgrounds, Christians gathered there to hear them from the turn of the century to the 1950s. Winona Lake was the Cadillac of all campgrounds.

Since the School of Theology operated only in the summertime, students came from all over the world because they did not need to sell their homes and move to the school's campus. They could study from the very best of professors in the world and complete their degrees during their summer vacations. The school offered a Master's and a PhD, accredited by Fuller Theological Seminary in Pasadena, CA, and London University in England.

The greatest Christian leaders in the world came to teach, not because of pay; they weren't paid much. They got a vacation for their family, their cabins had daily housekeeping and three meals were provided each day. While I was there, the school attracted the likes of Carl F.H. Henry, Kenneth Scott Latourette, O.J. Brown, Donald Guthrie, Kenneth Kantzer, Gleason Archer, etc.

"Tell me about that girl?" Dr. Latourette asked Sam at mealtime. We all fellowshipped around tables during meals. My son talked to the greatest scholars in the world about small things, about girls he thought were cute, and about the classic comics he was reading. Sam told them where they could find blueberries, raspberries, and blackberries.

At the same time these men intimidated me. I pedestalize men of greatness and had difficulty chatting with them. I always tried to talk to Dr. Latourette about his Lundensean theology, or how he arrived at his criteria for revival or some moot point of history.

St. Augustine said, "We must stand on the shoulders of those who have gone before and reach higher." That is what our children must do. They must stand on our experiences and reach higher levels in life. Let's not deprive them of their unique experiences, nor require them to feel our fears living within our limitations.

PRINCIPLES TO TAKE AWAY

1. The principle of learning to relax. Because many children have felt the fears of their parents, they are limited to the experience of those that have gone before them. As a result, they have not enjoyed the potential of a full life that could be theirs. Don't give them your fears that are not real. I didn't give Sam my intimidation of great men. On the other hand, sometimes fears are based in reality. We must communicate real fears to our children. If we didn't, we wouldn't be honest parents.

Sam was not afraid of these men; he was their friend. After their classes each day, they wanted relaxation. Sam provided it for them. Sam loved life, and they enjoyed being with him. He treated them like a grandpa; they treated him like a son. Sam got along well with the men that I respected. I should have played horseshoes with them instead of trying to impress them with my intellect.

2. <u>The principle of sanctified normality</u>. Sometimes we think that all of life should be lived at the high level of religious sanctification, living every moment to demonstrate our spirituality. We need to teach our children that the worth of life can be found in such activities as playing horseshoes, picking berries, or talking about girls. They need to know they can be spiritual doing these things. Twelve-year-old boys can enjoy playing horseshoes with PhDs. There was no academic relationship between the two, but at the same time there were no barriers between the two. Horseshoes was their common point of communication. They looked forward to playing horseshoes, they played horseshoes, and they enjoyed winning. And after all, it's important that we enjoy what we do, and we learn to win... or lose with the right spirit.

3. <u>A child shall lead them</u>. The three adults excelled in Christian leadership, but Sam was the best horseshoe player among them. The intellectuals liked Sam because he could do something better than they could—he could throw ringers. They all wanted Sam on their team, and whoever got Sam usually won.

"The child is father of the man," William Wordsworth is credited with saying. Among other things this statement means we can learn much from our children. We have all come from the world of children and we want to influence the world we have left. But the children can influence adults. Sam acted normal with the great intellectuals, and they acted normal with him. And I respect my son for that.

CHAPTER TEN

WORKING IN MEXICO:
A NEW HORIZON OF GROWTH

"Do you want to go to Mexico," I asked Debbie when she came home from school. "It'll be a week that'll change your life." I explained to her that it was not a vacation. She would work hard... probably all day into the evening.

"But," I explained, "It'll be the greatest week of your life."

Debbie had just turned fifteen years old and was finished with her second year of high school. She was the hardest working of the kids, also the most adventurous; she wouldn't be afraid of going to a foreign culture, eating different food and evangelizing a neighborhood with the gospel.

Roscoe Brewer, Youth Director of Kansas City Baptist Temple, was taking the highschoolers to Monterey, Mexico, for a week of missionary work. He was raising money to construct a church building and was taking along tradesmen from his church to supervise the work. The highschoolers would provide the manual labor and evangelize the neighborhood. Roscoe and his wife, plus six other couples were going down to the suburbs of Monterey. The ladies were counselors to help the young people to evangelize by passing out Bibles door to door.

Each day one-third of the kids would work manual jobs at the construction site, another one-third would pass out Bibles door to door, a final third would go "sightseeing" to understand Mexico, plus shop and swim. Obviously, the groups rotated their tasks each day. The kids slept at Camp Rio Escondido (Camp of the Hidden River). They learned to minister by ministering in Mexico, their accountability to God would grow by being accountable for a daily task. To me, the trip to Mexico was better than sending Debbie to a Christian camp where she would listen to Bible classes and have a vacation. She would learn a foreign culture by being immersed into its culture.

"You have to fly by yourself from Chicago O'Hare to Kansas City," I carefully explained to Debbie, then asked, "can you do it?"

"Sure... no problem."

"Then you will ride a school bus from Kansas City, Missouri, to Mexico," I cautioned how hot and tiring the ride would be. Then I asked, "Can you do it?"

"Sure... no problem."

"You will have to sleep each night in a sleeping bag, in a building that looks like a large screen porch," I explained to her. "Can you do it?"

"Sure... I'm a Towns," Debbie explained, "I can do anything."

I taught my kids the same thing that my mother taught me, "You are a Towns, you can do anything you put your mind to."

Debbie had to raise fifty dollars from individuals in our church by "selling" Bibles to the people. This helped pay for the Bibles and building supplies. Each time a person gave Debbie a dollar she put their name and mailing address on the front of a postcard, then when she distributed the Bible, the person who received it wrote their name on the back of the postcard. That way people back home prayed for Debbie and the people in the homes where the Bible was placed.

Working In Mexico: A New Horizon of Growth

"Can you raise fifty dollars for Bibles?"

"Sure... I'm a Towns... I can do anything I put my mind to."

There were over 150 kids on this expedition, Christian kids from Kansas City, Kansas, Lynchburg, Virginia, and Odessa, Texas. Being from different cities is where the tricky part came in. After Debbie flew by herself to Kansas City, she would ride a school bus to Mexico with kids she didn't know. During that week Debbie was in Mexico, Ruth and I, and the kids moved our home from Deerfield, Illinois, to Lynchburg, Virginia. I was moving to help Jerry Falwell start a new college which would be known as Liberty University. Debbie would have to ride back from Mexico to Lynchburg with a different group of kids. That meant she had to make new friends in Mexico from Lynchburg, Virginia, and be transferred to new adult supervisors to bring her back to us in Virginia.

Debbie is a trooper. If any of our kids can do anything, make anything happen, and rise to any occasion, Debbie is the champion. So, I wasn't worried about her, but I just wanted to make sure that everything was alright.

I did not dare drop her off at the front gate of O'Hare Airfield in Chicago. I went with her to the plane and made sure that the plane took off before I left the airfield. Then, I was not satisfied until I got a long-distance call from Kansas City that she had been picked up at the airfield. They told me she was on a bus heading for Mexico.

"I know everyone wants to pass out Bibles," Roscoe Brewer, the youth director announced that first day. But he pleaded with them, "I'll need some of you to volunteer for manual work on the building." Debbie was the first to put up a hand. She was willing to do anything.

When the jobs got sorted out, they handed Debbie a shovel and taught her how to mix concrete. Being in a primitive society, they couldn't phone for cement trucks to deliver concrete for the large church. With a shovel, young people mixed together cement, rocks and gravel, mixing it to the right texture called "mud." There were six groups of highschoolers mixing "mud" to lay the large concrete floor.

Out of several boys mixing concrete for the floor, Debbie was the only girl. According to Roscoe, she was better than any of the boys. But there was one problem, Debbie wore a dress. Even before going to Mexico, the girls were told they couldn't wear pants. It was not an American church thing, nor was it a modesty issue. In Mexico, only the prostitutes wore pants or slacks, all of the women wore dresses, even those who worked in the fields. Roscoe told her, "You got to mix concrete with a dress," he explained as gently as he knew how.

"Can I pull the back of my dress up between my legs and tuck it in my waistband like the ladies do in the fields," Debbie asked.

"Yes."

Working all day, they got the entire church floor poured and smoothed. One of the men was a concrete finisher, making sure that the job was as smooth as any commercial job in America.

"Smooth as poured milk," he boasted.

Everyone heard how hard it was to mix concrete, so the next day when Roscoe asked for volunteers, no hand went up.

"Come on you guys ...," Roscoe pleaded with the young people.

"I need someone to mix cement because we are laying concrete block today."

Debbie's hand went up.

A couple of embarrassed boys also put up their hands and worked with her that day preparing concrete for the block layers. Since they didn't need as much concrete for laying block as they needed for the entire floor, they only needed one gang making concrete, with the young people taking turns. Later, Debbie explained the process to me, "We call it two-piling. You begin with two piles, one of cement, the other of sand. You pull some cement into the center and mix it with water, then from the pile of sand you mix it together."

"Wasn't it hard work," I asked.

"Nah....," Debbie responded. "I liked it... I love to work; I am a Towns."

They kept Debbie two-piling concrete all week because she liked it and no one else volunteered. While I was happy that she was used in a crucial area, I was disappointed she did not get an opportunity to pass out Bibles as much as the other kids. On the last afternoon, she did go door to door passing out Bibles, filling out her postcards, then mailing them back to the people in the states that supported her.

After the concrete block walls were up, the men erected rafters and a roof. Many of the young people nailed together slats for benches to sit on, then nailed on backs. They were called "pews." Working from early Monday morning till the middle of Saturday afternoon, the workmen and young people from America constructed a church and pews. The first Gospel meeting was set for Saturday night. In America, the church probably seated between 100 to 125, but Mexicans have a way of packing pew that Americans have never thought of. They had over 250 in the building, standing around the walls, sitting in the aisles and gathered around open windows.

The young people formed a choir and memorized three or four songs in Spanish. There were no American pianos, but Roscoe Brewer had brought microphones, amplification and speakers. Young people sang to music tracks, and for three nights before the Saturday night Gospel service, the loudspeakers were directed down the streets to tell the people the type of music that would be sung in the gospel service.

"Come tonight and hear 100 Americans sing in Spanish," was the invitation.

As the American highschoolers went door to door inviting people to the Saturday night Gospel service, the neighborhood found it hard to believe the church building would be finished in five days. It took them about a year to build a building. But they came to see the swarming pale skin youth who worked harder than they had ever seen. There was always a crowd of neighbors watching them build the new church building.

All Saturday afternoon, the young people went from house to house inviting everyone to come, "hear 100 young people sing... 100 gringos sing Mexican style..."

"I've never been in a church service like that," Debbie described the atmosphere of the meeting. People came in smelly work clothes, some well dressed, others came dressed in what they were. Dogs wandered in the open door, chickens and the crowd didn't know how to act at a church service. They were more used to a bull fight or a rock concert.

Roscoe taught them choruses, singing in Spanish to soundtracks... loudly.

Debbie said she couldn't sing so she didn't volunteer for the choir. She and some other girls went to the bus to pray. One after another they cried out to God,

"Save souls ..." They wept for lost people.

"God use the preacher and give him power...," another prayed fervently.

"God use the music and singing...," still another wept.

I have always wanted my children to have a heart for evangelism. Of all of the times my children had been with me to crusades where I preached, they would have never gotten the passion for lost people like Debbie got in Mexico. I was not in that school bus to hear her pray, or to see her tears; but if I had witnessed it, I would have cried too. My prayers for God to work in Debbie's life were being heard and answered.

The best way to minister to your children is to get them ministering to others. The best way to get your children to grow in Christ is to get them helping others to grow in Christ. The old adage is still true, "You never learn a lesson better than those you teach to others." So now we can add, "A person never has their spiritual needs met better, than when they help someone else with those same needs."

"For God so loved the world, that He gave His only begotten Son," Roscoe began his sermon to a crowd of 250 Mexicans at that new church that night. The smell of wet concrete still permeated the building. But to that was added the barnyard smell of chickens, dogs, and laborers straight from their jobs. The crowd quieted when they heard,

"Porque de tal manera amo Dios al mundo que ha dado a su hijo unijento," the Spanish interpreter followed right behind Roscoe quoting John 3:16 in the language of the listeners.

"Daddy...," Debbie exclaimed when she got home. "Over 80 people came forward to get saved," Debbie babbled with enthusiasm when she got home at the result of the first night of evangelistic crusades.

The following morning, Debbie and the young people didn't attend that small church, but rather went to downtown Monterey to the large Baptist Temple because the sermon would be translated into English for them. Roscoe wanted them to experience a normal Mexican church service. Everyone was squeaky clean for the downtown church. Debbie and the kids bathed in Hidden River early Sunday morning.

That morning, only about thirty people came to the new little church that had been built the previous week. Even though 80 people made decisions the previous evening, less than half of them came back Sunday morning. Some didn't understand the implications of their decisions, others had to work and others were not ready to make a break from the Roman Catholic church.

Over the next two years, Roscoe Brewer kept me, and Debbie informed about the little Baptist church in the suburbs of Monterey, Mexico. Debbie remained interested because she had helped to build it. Since she spent most of her time "two-piling concrete," she looked at sections of the floor and considered it "hers." She looked at the concrete block wall and knew it was her cement that held the walls together. There was one pew there that she built by herself, so she called it, "Debbie's Pew." When no one else was looking, she went and sat on that pew and prayed for all of the unsaved people in the future that would sit in that pew.

"God, use this pew to get people saved," she asked.

Two weeks after I put Debbie on a plane from Chicago, Illinois, she arrived back in Lynchburg, Virginia, via a Thomas Road Baptist Church bus. They had driven straight through, over 36 hours on a hot school bus from Monterey, Mexico, to Virginia.

"Wasn't it hard?" I asked her.

"Nah..." was her only answer. "We slept all over the bus."

She described how they slept on their sleeping bags in the aisle, and under the seats. In several places they piled up suitcases on top of the seats, high enough for a flat spot to stretch out and sleep.

"We slept all the way home," she explained they were so tired.

Little events are remembered more by children than adults. Debbie remembers arriving in a strange town, i.e. Lynchburg, Virginia. She had never been there before. She didn't know anyone except the high school kids with her on the bus. And we were not there to meet her.

It's not that Ruth and I were uncaring parents. We didn't know what time the busses were arriving from Mexico. So, Debbie had to wait two hours late one evening in the church parking lot till someone told us she was in Lynchburg. Even then we didn't have a home, we were living in a motel.

Debbie was not afraid, but she liked to boast that at age 15 she was resourceful and could look after herself.

"Tomorrow morning you begin counseling at a Christian camp," I told Debbie when Ruth and I finally got to the church. I had signed her up to be a counselor at Treasure Island Youth Camp. She went from one place of serving God to another.

"I didn't realize you would be so tired," I apologized. When I told her she could get out of the counseling job, she explained,

"I can do it," she said with a smile. "I am a Towns' and I can do anything I set my mind to."

PRINCIPLES TO TAKE AWAY

1. <u>The principle that your will (volition) controls your life</u>. Many people in life don't rise to the challenges because they think that they can't do it. Others seem to always surpass their goals, because of their indomitable will, "they can do what they set their minds to do." Every child should be taught the proper exercise of willpower. When we allow children to surrender to their selfish desires, weariness, or give into inconveniences, they live their whole life at a low level. But when we teach children to believe in themselves, they can live beyond their abilities.

2. <u>The principle of pride in a family name</u>. My mother taught me, "You are a Towns, you can do anything." So naturally I taught the same principle to my children. "Be proud of the family name." I did not see all the things that Debbie did in Mexico, but if I had been there, I would have been proud of her; because she exhibited pride in the Towns' family name.

3. <u>The principle that different abilities contribute to soul winning</u>. Many people think that God cannot use them in evangelism to win other people to Christ, because they are not good salesmen. But people with different talents can be used in evangelism when they faithfully exercise the gifts God has given to them. Those who pass out invitations to gather a crowd to a Gospel service are just as vital in soul winning as the Gospel preacher who presents the message. Those who construct the church building are just as vital as those who sing in the building. Debbie learned to give God what she had. While she spent most of her time "two-piling concrete" and building a pew, she also prayed in the bus and felt just as responsible for winning people to Jesus Christ as the other youth who sang and were the soul winners at the altar.

CHAPTER ELEVEN

PRAYING FOR A MUSEUM:
SHARING SPIRITUAL LESSONS

I was sitting on the platform of the college orientation service. The dynamic speaker had challenged young people to make a checklist of their purpose in life. The speaker had asked, "What plans do you have for your life? Can you write down on a sheet of paper what you want to do for God?" And then he reversed the question, "Can you write down what God wants you to do?" Several young people came to the altar during the first verse of the invitational hymn. I could feel the presence of the Lord. I sensed God working in lives.

Then I saw the young man rise, there was determination in the way he stood. He was sitting halfway back on the left side, and as he made his way to the center aisle, I could tell that he meant business with God. Reaching the center aisle, he turned right and strolled assuredly to the front. There was a steel glint in his eye. There was no smirk, no embarrassment, and no hesitation. I immediately jumped from my chair and went to the front of the auditorium to meet him.

He was Sam Towns, my only son.

"Why have you come forward," I asked Sam. It was a question that I had asked hundreds of people at the altar on many occasions. I have always asked that question because I wanted the person coming forward to make a commitment of purpose. I have found over the years that when I get people to articulate what they want from God, I have a better chance to help them. My son was no different, I wanted to help him, so I said,

"Why did you come forward," I said to Sam putting an arm around his shoulder, hugging him briskly. We knelt together. He didn't cry, but neither do I cry when I show resolution. My son is like me; we are both emotional, but not the crying type.

"God's calling me to serve Him," Sam said in confidence.

"How do you know that God is calling you?" It was a question that I had asked many times before.

"When I couldn't write on a sheet of paper what I wanted to do," Sam explained to me. "I had to face the fact I didn't know what I wanted to do..."

Then Sam began to explain that he'd always had a sense that God was calling him, but he wasn't sure. He didn't want to go into full time service just because his father was in full time service. He didn't want people to think that he was just copycatting his father. He explained to me,

"I wanted to be absolutely sure it was God's call, and not just something that I decided to do."

We prayed together, and then hugged one another several times. Some of Sam's friends came around to congratulate and encourage him in his commitment. Faculty members from the college also came over to shake his hand and share words of encouragement with him.

I had been very careful all of my life not to push my son into full time service. Sometimes fathers talk about their sons becoming preachers or talk about their sons taking over their job... these fathers are planting subconscious seeds in their son's thinking, but they always add an exclusionary clause, ... if, or ... should God call him. I had never knowingly done anything like that; I felt that it was unfair to put that kind of pressure on my son to become a minister. Obviously, I had prayed and asked God "THY will be done." I was committed to whatever God wanted done. This night was the crowning achievement in a pastor's life, his son surrendered to do what God had called him to do. HIS son surrendered to serve Jesus Christ in full-time Christian service.

"Let's go out and get something to eat," I said when the crowd was almost gone from the meeting. We went to a local Denny's restaurant because they stayed open all night. As we sat at the restaurant, I shared with Sam the verses that God used to call me into His service. I also shared with him the incidence in my life of how I knew it was God's will for me to be a preacher.

"Tonight," Sam tuned his thoughts to the service we just heard, "the preacher said we should be able to write down on a sheet of paper what we wanted to do for God." Then he asked, "Can you write down on a piece of paper what you want to do for God in the future?"

POW!!!! That was quite a question. If it had come from another preacher, or even a layman, it would have been a challenging question. But from my son, the question was even more awesome.

"There are some things I dream about," I said to Sam. "Some of these I have not even shared with your mother."

Then I began to talk about what I wanted to do for God and what I wanted God to do for me. I took a Denny's napkin, spread it out flat on the table and made a list of five items I wanted to do.

1. Write a systematic theology.

2. Get an earned doctor's degree.

3. Begin a Sunday school museum.

4. Begin a Christian newspaper.

5. Write Bible study books, rather than just books on Sunday school methods and evangelism.

I had talked about some of these things with my wife. Other items I had discussed in messages, such as telling ministers in sermons that I wanted to write a systematic theology textbook. But I had never been forced to actually write them down in bold letters for everyone to see. But there were five statements written out on a napkin for people to read. They were no longer hidden in the recesses of my heart; I was now accountable because everyone could see them.

"Wow," Sam responded when he saw the five points. "You want to build a Sunday school museum..."

There were five items on the list, but the only one that caught his attention was the Sunday school museum. He knew I wrote books and he knew I liked to preach and teach the Bible. But there was a natural reason why the Sunday school museum caught Sam's eye. We had been living for the last two years in Savannah, Georgia, where the Chamber of Commerce claimed that the first Sunday school was started there.

Every textbook and encyclopedia claimed that the first Sunday school was started by Robert Raikes in Gloucester, England, in 1780. However, someone in Savannah found out that John Wesley taught the children of the Christ Episcopal Church in Savannah, and deducted that young Wesley began the Sunday school in that Georgia city.

In a downtown park of Savannah is the John Wesley oak. I remember as a small boy standing beneath that oak listening to my teacher saying, "Right here under this very tree, John Wesley began the first Sunday school." Since a teacher said it, it must be true, I thought. The same thing with Sam, since a teacher said it, he had to believe that it was true.

"What do you want to put in your Sunday school museum?" Sam began to question me. He got into the museum idea and wanted to put it in Savannah because of the claims of Chamber of Commerce.

I began to describe the articles that I felt ought to be in a Sunday school museum. It should include some of the very first Sunday school books, the charters that gave it existence and the artifacts from great Sunday school leaders of the past. I wanted to include photographs, Bibles, old chairs and desks, perhaps even some of the teaching tools.

"We ought to have a Sunday school Hall of Fame, with portraits of the great Sunday school leaders," I told Sam. That evening I mentioned there should be paintings of Robert Raikes, John Wesley and Francis Scott Key who wrote America's national anthem, but he also had a great influence on Sunday school.

"If we let the history of Sunday school die," I explained to Sam, "Bible teaching in our churches will die."

While I shared with my son my aims in life, it gave us a oneness in ministry. We were no longer father and son; we were co-workers together serving Jesus Christ.

"We ought to pray together for that list," Sam said, "especially pray about that Sunday school museum."

We finished our meal, paid, and went out to the car. In the front seat of the car we prayed for those five items. But it was more than praying for my list, we also prayed for Sam, for his calling and for God to use him in the Christian life. Sam was sitting in the front seat of that Chevrolet praying;

"Lord... Give my father a Sunday school museum," the sincerity of a transparent young Christian cannot be resisted by God. Sam continued praying, "Lord ... my daddy can build a greater museum than anyone else," he prayed, "because he loves Sunday school more than anyone else."

The next day I flew to Philadelphia, Pennsylvania, to speak to the city Sunday school convention. I arrived in town having taken an early morning flight and went straight to the old city municipal auditorium near the University of Pennsylvania. I arrived thirty minutes before having to deliver the message and went straight to the platform.

Looking over the schedule, I notice I spoke at 11:00 AM and was finished at noon. I didn't have another workshop until 4:00 PM, giving me over three hours to do some research. I knew that the American Sunday school Union was the oldest Sunday school organization in America and had many Sunday school artifacts in their headquarters. Since Sam and I had prayed the previous night about a Sunday school museum, I thought the American Sunday School Union office might be a good place to put feet to my prayers. That would be a good place to begin research for a Sunday school museum. I wanted to see what history the American Sunday School Union had on its walls. I felt that making a list of Sunday school artifacts around the world would be the first step in beginning the Sunday school museum.

I looked around the platform; the meeting was not ready to begin, even though the organ was playing. There were several members of the Philadelphia Sunday chool Convention standing there with me. I thought one of them might know where the office to the American Sunday School Union was located, and that they might have a car to drive me there. I saw Gerald Stover, a committee member and teacher at a Bible college. Since we had been friends, and shared many common concerns about Sunday school, I walked over to ask him,

"Do you know where the American Sunday School Union is located?" I asked. Stover was later to become an even closer friend. This portly man with a kind face, suddenly became ashen, his countenance dropped, and he said,

"Why do you want to know that, Dr. Towns?" Then he continued his explanation, "They closed their office downtown, and changed their name." He explained the organization dropped the name Sunday school from their title. Stover explained how the organization moved out of downtown Philadelphia into the suburbs. Stover told me that the items of Sunday school history that hung on their walls were thrown away. Their historical records were donated to the Presbyterian Historical Society.

"That's too bad," I let the words slowly drip from my lips. "I was going to start a Sunday school museum, and I knew that they had more memorabilia than any other place in the world."

Stover shook his head slowly, his eyes drooped. Without saying a word, I felt his sadness. I didn't know what to say. Everything Sam and I prayed for the previous night was gone. I felt like a man watching a train pull away from the station. I was too late.

"They threw most of that stuff away," Stover said to me.

"They threw Sunday school stuff away?" I said with a pained voice. I didn't honestly believe that anyone would throw away some of the most precious historical facts of life ... the history of the Sunday school.

"Yes, Dr. Towns," Stover explained. "When they dropped the name Sunday School from their title, they began throwing away all of the old Sunday school things they had hanging on the wall." Then Stover began to explain that they threw away pictures, plaques, charters, and Sunday school awards. They threw away boxes of old original Sunday school quarterlies. He explained that they threw away old plates from the original printing press, used to print Sunday school material. They threw away wooden blocks, small wood cuts, the ancient way of printing pictures in letter press equipment.

"Just last night, my son and I prayed about a museum..." I explained to Stover the conversation of how I listed the five dreams on a napkin.

"It was number 3 on my list." I pulled the napkin out of my Bible and showed it to Stover. Then pointing to the third item on the list, I said, "Last night we prayed for God to give me a Sunday school museum."

A little smile came to Stover's face. I didn't know what it meant. I didn't know if the smile meant he was glad to find someone else interested in Sunday school history. I didn't know if it was one of those little devilish grins that people have when they are playing tricks on one another. Then Stover explained to me,

"They threw everything in the trash can and set it on the curb for the garbage men to pick up," my friend slowly explained, "I backed my car up to the garbage cans and filled my trunk with memorabilia.

"Where is it?" I quickly spit out my words.

"At home in my basement."

"Could I see it?"

I went on to explain that I would like to come by his house and examine all of the materials.

"I will bring it for you tomorrow," Stover explained.

When Stover said, "I will bring it for you tomorrow," I didn't have any idea what he had in mind. I thought he would let me examine it and make an inventory of it for historical purposes.

I knew that God answered prayer, but I did not know that He answered that quick, nor did I know that He answered them that exactly. I had been serving the Lord for twenty-five years and no one had ever offered me any historical material on the Sunday school. Everyone knew I loved Sunday school, and everyone knew that I was interested in the history of the Sunday school. But in twenty-five years of ministry, no one had ever talked to me about a Sunday school museum. Then, one night I prayed about a Sunday school museum, and the next day I would hold it in my hands.

I had difficulty going to sleep that night. Not only was there anticipation in seeing the Sunday school material, but I was excited about answered prayer.

The next day Jerry Stover took me down into the garage basement underneath the city auditorium. It was two or three floors down by elevator. The parking garage was damp and dimly lit. Our footsteps echoed off of the concrete walls of the parking garage. When Stover opened the trunk, I eagerly stared in not knowing what I would see.

We looked like a couple of mafia hoods, examining their stolen goods in the trunk of a car.

"Dr. Towns," even though we were friends, Jerry always called me Dr. Towns. "Dr. Towns, I want to give all this to you."

I was speechless... I was grateful... I wanted to shout hallelujah... I was shocked. This was more than I could ever dream. This was more than I had asked of God. I knew that God gave exceedingly, absolutely, above all we ask or dreamed; but this was a gift too great to be believed.

"When I saw the napkin," Stover told me, "I decided in an instant to give it all to you." Jerry Stover believed in prayer and knew that he had what I had asked God to give me.

"This makes me the happiest person in life," Stover rejoiced with my excitement.

Jerry Stover had packed everything carefully in boxes so I could ship it back home with me to Georgia. There were dozens of little books used in Sunday school almost 200 years old. The printing press turned out to be an earlier version of the printing plate used today, although the off-set printing was done by marble plates. There were original wood cuts used in early printing procedures, and dozens of pictures, awards, and hymnbooks of all kinds.

"I didn't want to pack this," Jerry Stover handed me a gold dollar. "This is the 'Nellie Fox Dollar' that hung on the wall of the American Sunday School Union for over 100 years.

Stover pointed to the 1859 date on the one-dollar gold piece, that is about the size of a modern dime. Then he gave me a broken frame and the cardboard backing that had been in the frame. It told the story of Nellie Fox.

"They threw it out of the window thinking that it was not worth anything," he noted.

"It's very valuable as a collector's item," he explained that a coin collector would buy it. "But it has more value to you and me because we love the Sunday school."

Then Stover told me how Nellie Fox had attended a Sunday school rally where an appeal had been made for money to buy Sunday school books, to evangelize children in the wild west. The American Sunday School Union provided a library of one hundred books, to constitute a Sunday school. To pay for these books, Sunday school leaders asked Christians to help buy these books to win children to Jesus Christ. Nellie Fox was a little junior girl who heard the appeal and said, "My father gave me this dollar," she explained. "I want to give it to Jesus." Nellie Fox had given the money to help plant Sunday schools.

A wealthy man overheard the conversation and gave a dollar to the minister, then taking the gold minted dollar from the preacher, returned it to Nellie Fox saying,

"You ought to keep this because it was given to you by your deceased father."

"I didn't give it to you," Nellie told the kind gentlemen. "I gave it to Jesus to help children learn to read the Bible," she explained.

A Sunday school leader had traveled up and down the east coast of the United States holding up this dollar, using it as a symbol to raise money for Sunday schools in a project called the Mississippi Valley Enterprise.

"I'm not giving you this dollar," Stover explained to me. "You are holding the dollar in trust for Jesus," he explained, "use it for His glory."

I opened a Sunday school museum in Savannah, Georgia. From 1973 to 1978 it was located in Savannah as a testimony to all of the great historical influences of Sunday school. Today the historical artifacts and records are on file at the Jerry Falwell Library in Lynchburg, Virginia in the archives. They are available for all to read and/or research.

PRINCIPLES TO TAKE AWAY

1. The principle of effective prayers from elementary intercession. Sam was not educated in the principles of intercessory prayer, but he simply asked the Lord and God gave him what he wanted. He wanted a Sunday school museum for his Dad, and God gave it to him. Parents should realize the power when their children pray. Even when children do not understand as much Bible as they do, or are as mature as they are, or have the experience in intercession as they have, their simple faith is sometimes greater than educated faith.

2. The power of conceived objectives. I had always loved history, I had always loved the Sunday school, and I had always studied the history of Sunday school. I had thought about a Sunday school museum but had done nothing about it. When I told my son what I wanted, it crystallized my thinking and focused our prayers. It makes me accountable to my dreams. Ever since I had become a Christian, I knew the Bible exhortation, "You have not because you ask not" (James 4:4). And even though I knew I had to ask to receive, I had not asked for a Sunday school museum. The result, I did not have a Sunday school museum. Our children can help us focus our requests or give purpose to our prayers. They can help us get the answers that we only dream about.

3. The principle of stewardship. The Nellie Fox dollar is not mine; I am only entrusted with its keeping. It belongs to the history of Sunday school and to all who have sacrificed for the ministry of Sunday school. The Nellie Fox dollar is like many other things that God has given to each of us. We hold our time, talents and treasures in trust for the Lord. When we get possessive, the Lord cannot use them, but when we use them for God, His ministry is expanded.

4. The principle of writing our objectives. All of us should write what we want to do for God, and what we want God to do for us. This is an exercise of putting our dreams into words and then sharing our vision with others. Writing our dreams motivates us to action, because the process of writing clarifies what it is we intend to do. But more than clarifies, it objectifies our aims. When we write it down, we know

what to do. Then, we become accountable to what we write. If we never write it down, and never tell anyone, we never have to do it. But when we write our dreams, we are accountable to do what we dream.

CHAPTER TWELVE

PICKING UP FIREWOOD:
DOING MORE THAN EXPECTED

"Do we hafta?" my eleven-year-old Debbie grumbled across the breakfast table. "Do we hafta...?" her voice pleaded.

"We need to gather up the firewood at the curb," I told my family at the breakfast table. "All the neighbors will be picking up the logs for the fireplace to burn in the winter."

It was late summer in Deerfield, Illinois. This greater Chicago suburb reached over 90 degrees on the thermometer and no one was thinking winter firewood... except me.

The utility company had severely trimmed the aging elm trees up and down Osterman Street where we lived. They were removing any trees close to the power lines. They mulched the leaves and branches and took the trash away. They cut the heavy limbs into fireplace length then left them strewed up and down the decaying concrete curbs of Osterman Street. The utility company knew the residents would pick them up for firewood and save them from hauling the limbs away.

"If we don't get them TODAY" I emphasized the necessity of haste. "... If we don't get them TODAY... the neighbors will get all of the firewood."

I tried to appeal to the selfish nature of us all. I wanted to explain to my children the need in life to protect the firewood that was ours.

"The elm trees are on OUR property," I explained. "The firewood is in OUR yard, and the firewood is in the street in front of OUR home."

"Do we hafta?" Debbie still resisted my plan. The firewood needed to be picked up that morning because our neighbors would soon be swarming into the streets like industry ants, to get the firewood for the coming winter.

"You do it, Daddy," my daughter was quick to shift the responsibility back to me. After all, most parents do what their children won't do and can't do.

I drew my lips into a facial response that said "no" long before my words said "no." Then I slowly shook my head from side to side saying, "I have to teach a class all morning..."

The breakfast table was silent except for scraping of forks over cheap ceramic plates, trying to scrape up the last of the scrambled eggs. I was trying to think up a way to motivate Debbie... the oldest... to want to pick up the firewood. I thought of the "family" argument. I told her,

"Think of the fun our family will have sitting in front of a laughing fire... sharing quality time... popping corn." I tried to exaggerate family enjoyment when the snow fell, and we'd be trapped indoors.

"I don't wanna," she pouted. "It's not fun to sit with my family..." She again slowly emphasized, "MY family" and said she'd rather be with her friends.

So much for my great idea to appeal to family togetherness and family fun. She was approaching age twelve, going on eighteen. She couldn't be motivated by family unity.

I faced the possibility of losing the firewood to the neighbors. I'd have to pay to bring a truckload of firewood for the winter. Debbie wasn't motivated by saving money. When I told her, I would have to pay fifteen dollars, she didn't care. She wasn't motivated by money, but I was. I hated to waste money.

Picking Up Firewood: Doing More Than Expected

"THAT'S IT!!" I thought.

I was motivated by money to get the firewood in my basement. I wanted to save money. It would cost me fifteen dollars for a load of firewood."

"WHY NOT PAY DEBBIE," I thought. Slowly I formulated a plan. I tried to imagine how many logs would fill up a pickup truck loaded with firewood. I pictured about 50 to 100 logs in the back of a pickup truck. So, if I paid Debbie a penny a log, it would cost me about fifty cents to get a pickup truck load of firewood tossed through the basement window into the cellar.

We didn't have a modern basement with concrete floors, drain and fancy lights on the ceiling. It had a musty-smelling dirt floor, with bugs in dark corners and crevices. The floor joints were exposed on the basement ceiling. Only one naked light bulb hung from the center cross beam.

"I'll give you a penny a log," I told Debbie and turning to Sam age nine, and Polly age seven, I repeated the offer. "I'll give you a penny a log."

Then to make sure there was accountability I added, "The log has to be thrown through the basement window."

Debbie didn't jump at the proposal of one penny a log. She was figuring out how much she would make. As Debbie was thinking about my proposition, Sam interrupted,

"Yea..." He was first to answer. "Yea... I'll do it."

"Me too..." the youngest Polly chimed into Sam's enthusiasm. "I'll get Beth to help me." Beth was Polly's best friend. They did everything together.

I was not trying to pit the oldest Debbie against her two younger siblings. But that's what happened. When Debbie saw Sam muscling in on her deal, she jumped to the occasion.

"I'll do it" she answered with authority.

A little squabble momentarily broke out among the children... They argued over who would get the smaller firewood... who would get the wood closest to the basement window... who would count?

I had what I wanted... the children would pick up the firewood... they would do it right away before the neighbors got to it... and they would stack it in the basement.

"Remember..." I carefully said, "I'll only pay a penny for each log in the basement."

"Three cents" Debbie bargained. "One penny for me, one penny for Sam, and one penny for Polly."

"No..." I cut off her misunderstanding. Knowing my children, I had to have a clear agreement before the work was done, not after.

"ONE PENNY FOR ONE LOG" I said very slowly and clearly. "NOT THREE PENNIES FOR EACH LOG."

Knowing Debbie was the bossy one, I put her in charge of keeping score. I knew she wouldn't let Sam and Polly count her logs, but I also knew Sam and Polly, wouldn't let Debbie cheat them.

"Let's go..." Debbie challenged her brother and sister. She stood to her feet and wiped egg off her face. She was ready to go gather firewood.

"Eat your breakfast first..." Ruth had to restrain them. A few minutes ago, I was trying to motivate them to do a little job, now we had to hold them back. I was learning a basic lesson in motivation. People don't enthusiastically do what YOU want them to do, they enthusiastically do what THEY want to do.

"If you finish the job," I told the kids, "I'll take you all for supper at McDonald's for hamburgers, French fries and Coke." Then I added, "But ya gotta finish the job to get McDonald's."

Picking Up Firewood: Doing More Than Expected

Our salary was marginal, so going to McDonald's was a big treat for the family. We ate most of our meals at home. There was nothing in the budget to eat out. Only when I got an honorarium for preaching did we have extra money to eat out. I thought the McDonald's incentive would make sure they didn't quit halfway through the job.

"Remember" I continued, "I'll pay a penny a log, but no McDonald's if you don't get at least 50 pieces of firewood in the basement.

I left for school and completely put the contract out of my mind. Not once all day long did I think about firewood in the basement. I usually got home around 3:30 in the afternoon. This particular afternoon was no different; and on my way home I still hadn't thought about the firewood. I didn't give it any thought as I drove up to Osterman Street.

There sitting on the curb were eight little rascals, sitting pretty... lined up in a row. They looked like some mother had lined them up on the curb and threatened them with mortal punishment if they didn't "sit perfectly still."

Debbie was sitting on the curb closest to the driveway, then Sam and the rest of the neighborhood kids, like a row of peas in a pod.

They were sitting still even though no one told them to sit still.

They were waiting anxiously for me to arrive, and the whole gang was crowded as close to our driveway entrance as possible. I saw them before they saw me. When they saw my car, they instantly sprang into action... yelling... waving... giggling.

As I turned in the driveway, they grabbed the car door handle. I had to stop, barely getting the car out of the street.

They were all yelling at me as they opened the car door and pulled me out of the front seat toward the back door of the house. That was the door that led to the cellar.

Polly had cupped her hand over her mouth and was trying to tell me a secret but couldn't. Some were pushing, some were pulling me toward the back door. By this time, I knew what had happened. They had 50 logs in the basement. I expected to open the door, peer down in the darkened basement to see 50 pieces of firewood stacked neatly against the wall under the basement window. I expected them to do just like I'd do it. I'd make a nice neat stack of firewood... the big pieces of firewood on the bottom and the little pieces on top.

I stared into the darkened basement but couldn't see anything. I squinted out the summer sunlight, but I still couldn't see the dirt floor. The flood seemed a blur. I couldn't see the dirt.

"Turn on the light" Debbie laughed over the other giggling children. I reached across the hall to flip the switch and turned around to the uncontrollable laughter of eight children.

I still couldn't see the floor; it was covered with firewood. I couldn't see the bottom of the stairs; it was covered with firewood.

Then it dawned upon me. As I drove home down Osterman Street, our yard was clear of firewood. So were the neighbors' yards. There were no logs in the yards on both sides of our house and across the street.

All the logs were in my basement.

I laughed and hugged the kids. The kids laughed and hugged back.

They dropped so many logs through the basement window, they covered the basement stairs and basement floor. They hadn't stacked the logs, just piled them on the floor. So, I said nothing about stacking the logs. They hadn't stacked the logs like I would have; they were just kids. Later I threw the firewood under the stairs. There were just too many to stack.

"Are you going to share your money with the neighborhood kids?" I threw out a question to the gang of kids standing around the back door.

"YEA!!!" they all screamed.

I didn't want to get into an argument about who got the money. Nor, did I want to become the judge to determine how much each one got. So, I came up with an idea that would reward them all.

"I'll take you all to McDonald's for supper."

"YEA!!!" they screamed again.

The neighborhood kids got involved early in the morning. Debbie, Sam and Polly were picking up one or two logs at a time, walking over to the basement window and pitching them into the darkened floor. The walk was taking too much time and little Polly was getting tired. Since, the innovative can always find an easier way to do a job quicker, Debbie coaxed some helping out of her playmates and those who came to play with Sam and Polly. She lined them up like a bucket brigade at a fire. They passed the logs from one to another. When the line stretched to the street or to a neighbor's yard, they threw the logs to one another. They didn't try to catch the firewood but picked it up and threw it on toward the basement window.

There were 305 logs in my basement, costing me over three dollars. I tipped each of the kids and we went to McDonald's.

PRINCIPLES TO TAKE AWAY

1. The principle of rewards. This principle is basic to dealing with children, youth and adults. When people get rewarded, they get things done. Only five percent of our population will work diligently without pay at a task because of their character. Ten percent will work diligently when no one is watching, just because a job needed to be done. However, 85 percent of people work because they expect something in return.

At first, I was wrong in the way I tried to motivate Debbie. I expected little children to work willingly, displaying character that I had not yet inculcated in them. They were too little to learn the dignity of hard work. Since character is habitually doing the right thing in the right way, I needed to train them to work hard before I expected them to work hard. They were not old enough to have developed proper work habits that I as an adult had developed from my mother.

2. <u>The self-incentive principle of motivation</u>. Debbie didn't want to do a lot of hard work for quality family time around a friendly fire. She wanted to be with her friends. When I appealed to her self-incentive to earn money, I caught her attention. I motivated her to action.

3. <u>The immediacy principle of motivation</u>. Children have short attention spans. It is easy to harness their energies for the immediate future. But, it's hard to get children to take a long look. To children, time moves slowly, and little ones have so little experience on which to make future judgments. Therefore, they judge the whole world by what they know. They know the present and are motivated by the present.

I tried to motivate Debbie with next winter's warm fire, while it was 90 degrees in greater Chicago. When it's hot in Chicago, or any place, children look for cool places and they don't like to work in the sun. They look for immediate enjoyment, not postponed gratification.

4. <u>The principle of making work enjoyable</u>. Children like to do what is fun. When they think it's hard or unpleasant, they don't want to do it. They don't like to work. Yet fun is measured by attitude, not by sweat, toil, pain and exhaustion. Most children have chosen to hate work. However, kids love to run hard, get dirty playing football, jump rope and ride a bicycle till they are tired. These things are fun, because they have chosen to have fun playing the games. But they complain when they have to get dirty cutting the grass or get sweaty working in the garden. It's not fun clearing the table, making several trips from the dining room to the kitchen. We could help our kids gain maturity by teaching them there is a difference between getting tired playing baseball and getting tired cutting grass. If they chose to have fun working hard, it'll be enjoyable. If we teach them to enjoy work, we've taught them to enjoy life.

5. <u>The principle of goal-oriented labor</u>. When I challenged the

Picking Up Firewood: Doing More Than Expected

kids to pick up 50 pieces of wood, promising to reward them with McDonald's, I was teaching them to work till a job was done. Now honestly, I wanted the yard clean, but the by-product was to teach children to keep working till they finished a job.

And WOW!!... did they finish. Instead of cleaning up our yard, they cleaned up several neighbors' yards.

CONCLUSION

Children will do what we reward, so let's give them rewards when they work hard. Don't challenge them too high; it will discourage them. A low goal will insult them. Since children get things done that they enjoy, make their work fun. Also, that which is immediate is conceivable in the minds of children, so give rewards immediately when they attain their goals.

Children are not adults in little bodies that can be motivated by adult reasons. They are what they have grown to be, and they will be what we motivate them to do.

CHAPTER THIRTEEN

"B-U-T-T": YOU CAN'T SAY THAT

The family was sitting at the dining room table, we had already finished dinner; just sitting around talking about everything and nothing in particular. Ruth was finishing her cup of coffee, and I was reading the sports page. Debbie, a young teen was telling Sam and Polly what it was like to be in high school. I was not listening to them, rather I was focusing on the Chicago Cubs. Then my subconscious heard Debbie say,

"She hit me in the butt..."

"WHAT!!!" I dropped the paper, looked up in astonishment at what I had just heard. The kids knew that response, they froze and stopped talking. All eyes were looking at me. Not knowing exactly what Debbie had said; I thought I heard the B word.

"NO... NO... NO..." I repeated myself, "We don't say that word in our family." Then glancing from one set of eyes to the next I again repeated, "We don't say the B word." I just said the first letter of the word so I wouldn't say it.

I was naive when it came to my children. For some reason I thought my children would be vastly superior to all other children. I thought that when they heard an inappropriate word at school, they would never repeat it. I thought when my children saw something evil, they would never want to try it. And I thought when my children experienced any form of sin, they would be repulsed by it.

Was I naive... did I have a lesson to learn about life?

When it came to my daughters, I wanted them to be refined southern young ladies. I had an image in my mind of a cultured, genteel, young southern belle. I had an image of girls who always wore dresses, never got their hands dirty, and never broke out in a sweat. Obviously, I had seen my children play in the backyard, coming in the house with mud from top to bottom. So I knew that my children were like other children, they got dirty, they fought and they perspired. But I thought sure that none of my girls would ever say the word, "butt."

"Young ladies do not say B-U-T-T." I spelled it out for Polly and Debbie. I went on to explain, "This is a word that worldly people use, we do not use it."

"We do not say that word because Christians would be offended if you use that word ..." I explained to the girls the Christian standards of talking about different parts of the body, i.e., sexual parts of the body. Those words were not said or were not even mentioned. Then I pulled out my "Rook" card, the one I always used to remind our kids that they had a higher standard than anyone else,

"Remember you are the children of a preacher," I explained, "and people expect higher standards of us than anyone else."

The girls did not always agree with that explanation, but they understood the implications of it. The kids had many advantages because they were the children of a preacher, they got taken to the finest restaurants, they got vacations at the finest places, and they were treated much nicer, just because they were my children. So, I reminded them that along with the advantages there were some disadvantages. You have to live up to the expectation of other people.

"But everybody at school calls it a B____," Debbie didn't say the word, but she just used the first letter. Then she looked from Ruth to me to see if it was alright to identify it by its first letter.

"I don't care what anyone says," I was firm with the girls. "We don't say that word." Then I explained,

"We are different, our vocabulary is different, and we can not say words that others use."

"People who are Christians may use the word B-U-T-T," I spelled it out. "Because they do not know any better. But you are Christians. You cannot use that word."

"Then what do you call it?" Debbie asked. When she used "IT," we all knew what she meant because she pointed to "IT."

"Hmmm ...," I paused to come up with the right answer. We all started laughing. Someone said, "Can we call it, tush?"

"Can we call it, behind?"

"Can we call it, seat?"

"Can we call it by its proper name," Debbie asked. "Can we call it a buttock?"

We all laughed at the technical word BUTTOCKS. It just didn't sound right in everyday language. Sam chimed in,

"The hard church pews hurt my BUTTOX." He distinctively used the word "buttocks" slow, pronouncing each syllable.

We had lived five years in Canada, and the Canadians had a descriptive term for it that was different than anything we had ever heard. The Canadians called it a "bum." I have no earthly idea how it became a "bum" but that term was used by most everyone, from small children right up to preachers; so I guess that was alright.

"Shall we call it 'bum'?" One of the kids said. "If we do, Americans will think we are weird..."

Everyone in the family knew that they could not use the "A___" word. That was definitely out because it was a term used in cursing. Even though it was used in the Bible to describe a donkey, I would not even use the "A____" word when referring to a donkey or jackass in preaching.

Our conversation went from the B-U-T-T word (I was careful to spell it) to other words that Christians could not use.

None of the kids were allowed to watch the Saturday morning cartoon *Beany and Cecil*, because they used a word that I felt was a minced oath, which was a replacement for a cuss word. I explained to the kids that they could not watch Beany and Cecil because they used the D-A-R-N word.

"Why?" Polly asked.

"The D-A-R-N word (again I spelled it) is really a replacement for the D__ word, a four-letter word used in cursing." God had prohibited us from taking His name in vain or blaspheming. When we use the D word, we were condemning someone to hell which was a prerogative that only God could do.

"What the heck..." was another thing Beeny and Cecil said that we didn't want the kids to use. The word "heck" was a minced oath of the word Hell, and they couldn't use Hell in their terminology.

As a little girl, Ruth had said the word "golly" which is a minced oath for God. When Ruth said that her mother slapped her face, not hard to hurt it, but a pat on the mouth that she was not to use that word. A few years later in junior high, Ruth came home and said another word. Her mother was horrified. She took a bar of Fels Naphtha laundry soap, marched Ruth into the bathroom and said,

"Bite," she demanded.

"Now chew..."

With tears in her eyes, Ruth was forced to chew soap until the suds came. When the saliva foamed suds in the mouth she was allowed to spit it into the sink. It was Ruth's mother's way to teach her not to say bad words or even questionable words.

PRINCIPLES TO TAKE AWAY

1. The principle that words are thoughts. It is important what children say and not say, because the words we speak represent the thoughts of our hearts. Ruth always quoted to the girls, "Let your speech be always with grace, seasoned with salt" (Col. 4:6). Technically, the words come from our thinking heart, and the way to change our words is to change our heart. But at the same time, when we reverse the process by cleaning up our words, we give attention to keeping a pure heart. Since only God can purify and change the heart, by watching what we say, we are symbolically asking God's help with what we think and what we become.

2. The principle that our words are seeds of character. When we are training children, we are planting character seeds into which they shall grow. By teaching them what words they can say, and what words they cannot say; we are planting proper seeds for character formation. Character is defined as habitually doing the right thing in the right way. Therefore, we want them to habitually say the right words in the right way.

3. The principle that words mold our self-perception. Those who use negative words, are building up a negative self-image. When they see themselves in a negative light, they begin living by that influence. Children who use rebellious words, are influencing the heart to rebel against doing the right thing in the right way. Kids pick up bad words from their friends, from the environment, from the media, and out of their own sinful heart. Therefore, it is important that parents monitor their children's language, correct their word usage, and give children reasons why certain phrases cannot be used.

4. The principle of family standards. At one time, parents could say to the children, Christians don't use that language. However today, many Christians use all types of words, phrases, and terminology, using them without guilt or thought. I once said to a Christian worker,

"You can't say C-R-A-P," spelling out the word for him. He laughed at me and said,

"It's alright to say; it doesn't mean anything."

The Christian worker was wrong. While it didn't mean anything to him and was an innocent word, the word brought images of human waste and feces to other people. Older Christians remember when it was a nasty, word to describe something filthy. Can a Christian use words that have no meaning to them, but are offensive to others? We have to ask,

"Am I my brother's keeper?"

Just because some believers use certain words, that does not make it right. So, I had to appeal to my children, "You are a Towns, and I expect better out of you." Just as my mother told me when I was a small boy, "You are a Towns," so I tried to instill that same standard in my children. While some Christians may use questionable standards, we have to instill a higher standard in our children.

CHAPTER FOURTEEN

REMLE NOEL:
SINGING WHO YOU ARE

The family was packed in our white Chevy impala, driving across northern Minnesota on our family vacation. The kids, who usually fought over backseat turf, were quietly reading in the back seat. Even though I wanted them to enjoy the world we were exploring, they were not looking out at the unfolding passage of pine trees and rolling hills. Our Chevy pulled easily at the two-lane highway slowly gliding over hill after hill. Out of boredom, Debbie leaned forward, put both elbows over the front seat and asked,

"Can we listen to some of our music?"

"No."

I was listening to my music which could be described as... slow... melodious... a ballad. When the kids listened to their music, it was... loud... unintelligible... raunchy. I had a rule that whoever drove the car got control of the radio, and I didn't like the kid's music, so I listened to mine. When Ruth drove, she let them listen to their music. They listened to junk stuff... at least what I call junk stuff... Elvis Presley, the Beatles, or some other wailing voices and loud guitars.

"Do you like that?" Debbie said, pointing to the radio. I was listening to a slow ballad, that could be described as simply a love song.

"Yuck!"

"I like it...," I let my words out slowly because my taste was just as important as hers.

"Do you know who sings that song?" Debbie turned inquisitive.

"No."

"She's one of my singers, not one of your singers," Debbie explaining that the singer was not who I thought it might be.

"Oh yeah?"

"Describe to me what this singer looks like," my daughter challenged me. Debbie knew the singer was Mama Cass Elliot. I had never heard of Mama Cass Elliot, I had only enjoyed the song that she was singing, it was a beautiful love song that touched my heart.

"Stars shining bright above me,

Breeze softly whispers I love you,

Birds singing in the sycamore trees,

Dream a little dream of me."

I like this song because it reminded me of the music I sang in my youth. It reminded me of the 1940's and 50's. It was the kind of music I sang when I fell in love with my wife. I knew theoretically that everyone enjoyed music that they listened to when they went through puberty and adolescence. In a sense, the music that influenced their personality, is the music they identified with for the rest of their life. When someone was finding their self-perception, that kind of music would define their person when they were adults. The song, "Dream a Little Dream of Me," by Mama Cass was identifying music that I sang in my teenage years. Debbie saw the look in my eye; she asked me again,

"The song says, 'Dream a little dream of me,' so describe what this girl looks like to us."

When Sam and Polly heard the conversation, they leaned forward putting their elbows over the front seat. They knew what Debbie was doing, but I didn't. We were a huddled mass toward the front seat of our car, I was driving, the kids were hanging over the front seat and Ruth sitting beside me was intently listening. My wife joined in with the children, she knew what they were doing.

"Yeah," she egged me on, "I want to know what this girl looks like that you're dreaming a little dream of."

I thought for a minute and began to describe what I thought the female singer looked like, at least I described what she looked like in my mind ... her voice sounded beautiful, so I knew she was beautiful. Her voice sounded skinny, so I knew that she was skinny. After thinking about it a moment, I began describing the female singer to the kids.

"She's a young girl... slim... with black hair combed into a flip." I thought about it and began to describe her clothes, "she's dressed in a blue pleated skirt, and a white blouse." I pondered a minute and added, "She's wearing saddle oxfords, black and white."

"Does she look like a cheerleader?" Ruth interrupted my dream of Mama Cass who was doing the singing.

"Yeah."

When I said "Yeah" the kids let go of the front seat, rolled into the back seat, erupting into hilarious shouts of laughter. The laughter was so explosive; I saw Sam holding his side in pain as the he laughed at my naivety. That was before the days of high fives, but the kids were congratulating each other. They had "put down" their dad who thought he knew music. All sibling rivalry disappeared in the back seat; they had put one over Dad. They were one... one in humor... laughing at their father.

"She's a slob." Debbie threw her description of Mama Cass into the front seat and continued laughing,

"She's a cow." Sam used the phrase to describe Mama Cass, long before Bart Simpson used cows to describe everything he wanted to put down.

"She's an elephant." Polly would not be out done.

Then Ruth began to describe Mama Cass' obese figure, her hippy-like ways, and then she told me about the singing group The Mamas and Papas. The Mamas and the Papas were a rock group. My beautiful singer was Mama Cass, a member of a rock group that I would not play on the car radio while I was driving. So, the kids brought me down to their level of music.

Our conversation became serious. I was one with them, because my adult wall had been breached. They entered the world of their dad, or rather to put it more descriptively, I had come down to their level in music. We were talking not as father to children, but as peer to peer. Then one of the kids asked, I don't know which kid asked the question, but they wanted to know a secret that I would not tell the members of the family.

I wrote poetry, and published poetry anonymously. I published my poetry under a pseudonym, or some people say a pen name. The kids knew I had a nome de plume, but I would never tell them. Once before, they had begged, and argued that they needed to know in case there was money coming their way in inheritance. There was no money. I was one of the editors of *Christian Youth Today*, and published poetry there and other places. Every time they asked, my answer was always the same,

"No."

But that afternoon in northern Minnesota, it was a different setting. They were not just kids, I thought; they were soon to be adults. The oneness I felt with them made me very vulnerable. Since the adult wall had been breached, and we stood on level ground, I began to melt.

"Come on and tell us..." They wanted to know the secret name I called myself.

"Okay... I'll tell you..."

I waited a moment and thought about the repercussions. Once the kids knew my pseudonym, they would always know. Once the feathers were spilled out of the pillow into the wind, I could never get them back. So, I gave it a few seconds of thought, then decided I would trust them but, I wanted to extract a promise from them first.

"I'll tell you what my pseudonym is," I reasoned with the kids as though they were adults. "But you have to promise me that you will never tell anyone my pen name, and that you will never breathe a word of this to anyone."

"I promise," said Debbie.

"Me too," said Sam.

"That's not good enough," I said to Sam. "I want to hear you say, 'I promise I will never tell anyone what your pseudonym is."

"I promise." Sam repeated all of the oath I asked.

Polly also promised.

And then letting the silence of the moment sink in on all of us, I then breathed out the name.

"Remle Noel." I waited a moment, and nothing was said. They didn't know what they heard. I repeated, "Remle Noel." Then to explain what they had just heard, I said,

"My pseudonym is Remle Noel." There was no response from Ruth, no response from the kids. Waiting another moment, I said, "That's my name spelled backwards. It is Elmer Leon spelled backwards."

Then the back seat exploded into laughter. The kids who had their arms hanging over the front seat listening to me, again rolled backwards into the back seat and elbowed one another in mocking humor.

"Remle," Debbie said.

"Remle Noel," Debbie laughed.

"Remle Noel." Each time she said it, Sam and Polly laughed.

It was not as though they made fun of my name, even though it was funny to them. "Remle Noel" had a poetic ring to it.

When the kids got home, the first thing they did was tell their friends that their dad published poetry under the name of Remle Noel.

Their friends laughed.

At that moment my pseudonym was never again used. I never again published poetry under the pseudonym of Remle Noel. As far as I was concerned, that day Remle was buried in the grave, a tombstone erected in his memory, he was never again seen.

Today I have another pseudonym and it was interesting how I arrived at this pseudonym. Back in the 70's I wrote a poem and wanted to submit it to a magazine. I was searching for a pen name when talking with a friend. In the conversation he mentioned his grandfather's first and second name, I liked it. So, returning home, I typed the name of my friend's grandfather at the top of my poetry and submitted it. Remle Noel had died, there lives a new poet in his place, he's not a great poet, he's not a memorable poet, nor is he a wealthy poet. He is an anonymous poet, and only I know who it is... it is me.

PRINCIPLES TO TAKE AWAY

1. The principle that kids are kids. There was a day in northern Minnesota when I treated my kids like adults, and I gave them some information as adults, thinking they could keep it secret as adults.

What I should have realized is that kids are kids, and if I realized that, Remle Noel Snwot would still be cranking out poetry in magazines. Technically, I had grown tired of the name Snwot, and I had shortened my name to Remle Noel. I thought it had a romantic ring, or at least a poetic ring.

2. <u>The principle of deceptive perception</u>. Many times, we perceive things in life, when in fact we are misleading ourselves. I thought that any music that sounded like my style of music would be sung by people who reflected my values in life, i.e. the values of the 1940's. Well, I was wrong. The music that I liked that was sung by Mama Cass, was sung by a woman who didn't reflect my values in her personal lifestyle. The problem is that when we like something, we tend to project our values on to it.

3. <u>The principle of family oneness</u>. There is within the heart of each member of a family, from father to mother to all of the children, the desire to have a harmonious relationship between all family members. When we experience that oneness in the Towns' family, it was one of those defining moments when we knew one another, trusted one another, and opened up our hearts to one another. Such was the moment in northern Minnesota when I felt confident to open up my heart to my kids. Even though my kids betrayed my trust that time, there were many other occasions when we experienced oneness. From those experiences of oneness, we became a family bonded together in purpose and love.

4. <u>The principle of defining music</u>. Most people sing music for the rest of their lives that they learned when they were defining themselves as a person. This usually happened during their puberty or adolescent years. It has been said that every generation sings music that irritates the generation that goes before them. Maybe that is because every generation is seeking to define themselves through the pressures of the culture they are experiencing. Since culture has been spiraling so rapidly in radical changes for the past 100 years, each generation defines itself differently from the previous generation. As a result, every generation tends to dislike the music of its kids and those who follow them.

CHAPTER FIFTEEN

THE MISSIONARY CLOSET: BACK DOOR TO THE BEST

"Ruth, will you help with the missionary closet," the dean's wife asked Ruth when we first moved to Chicago. I became associate professor of Trinity Evangelical Divinity School, at the time considered one of the prestigious seminaries in the country. Even though Trinity Evangelical Divinity School was well respected, I had stepped down from the position of president of Winnipeg Bible College. Even though there was less salary as a Bible college president than I got at Trinity, people treated the office of president with dignity, and expected me to live by an elevated style of life.

"Will you help gather clothes for the student wives," the dean's wife at Trinity asked my wife.

When I first heard about the request, I was not sure Ruth should do it. To me, she would be doing a "goodwill" job with little glamour. If anything, it was welfare work, and I still thought of Ruth as the wife of a college president, not a welfare worker.

Anyone could see we didn't have much of this world's goods. Our family was dressed clean and appropriate, but the north shore of Chicago was exclusive. We now lived among the "upper crust," but had little dough to hold it together. The dean's wife told Ruth,

"You'll get to keep some of the clothes for you and the children," she explained to Ruth, "that's how we pay you to do the job..."

The fact my wife would be wearing someone's "rejects" bothered me. "SUPPOSE WE MEET A LADY IN CHURCH AND RUTH IS WEARING HER LAST YEARS DRESS," I thought. As a man, I was supposed to provide for my wife. She was not supposed to rummage through someone's "hand-me-downs." I pictured my wife as a "bag lady."

"I'd love to do it," was Ruth's response. She had prayed about the ministry and felt it was a place where she could help the seminarian wives, she had been married to me as we went through Seminary, so she understood their money problems.

"Ladies will phone with donations of clothes," Ruth was told. "You'll go by their house to pick up the clothes, sometimes wash the clothes, sort them, and hang them in the missionary closet."

Ruth looked forward to the job as a ministry, my reaction is, "what will people think of me and my family?" I was concerned more about reputation than of helping other people. What I thought was a demeaning job, turned out to be a positive asset, something that helped us through our financial difficulties. It was God's way of giving us "Nieman Marcus" clothes when we couldn't afford a K-Mart "blue-light" special.

Trinity Evangelical Divinity School had moved from the North side of Chicago, Illinois, twenty miles farther north to the prestigious village of Bannockburn, a secluded town of mansions and country estates owned by the wealthy who commuted via Northwestern trains to downtown Chicago each day. These sophisticated ladies threw away clothes that were the best the Chicago Mercantile had to offer.

"Can you come by my house and pick up a couple boxes of clothes," the voice over the telephone told my wife. "I'll be home at 4:30 pm this afternoon..."

"I'll be there," Ruth responded.

When Ruth brought the boxes into our living room that night, she was dumbstruck. She had no idea how expensive the clothes would be. She said, "You'll never believe what's in the box of clothes. Some of the dresses were never worn, others she only wore one time." Ruth holding up a dress, said it was over $400. It was a new designer dress that had only been worn to one reception.

That evening Ruth tried on dress after dress, suit after suit, coat after coat ... she was in heaven with skirts, blouses and things that were better than she had seen in years.

"I can't keep them all...," Ruth reasoned. She knew the seminarian wives were just as poor as she was. The clothes were given to seminarian wives, not to us. But at the time I not only taught full-time at Trinity Evangelical Divinity School, I was a student at Garrett Theological Seminary; so technically, I qualified as a poor seminarian.

"I'll keep just one or two," Ruth explained that she was going to keep a dress and suit. But she felt guilty about keeping anything.

"How much do you think I should keep?" She asked me.

After giving it some thought and discussion, we came up with the following formula.

> 1. Don't take the very best.
>
> 2. Don't take all of the best.
>
> 3. Don't take only the best.

Ruth received many boxes of children's clothes, because little ones constantly grew out of last year's fittings. And the boxes were filled with children's clothes that were the best that money could buy. Ruth brought home a school dress for Debbie, and for Polly, an outfit for gym class. There were even a few things for Sam. Eventually, Ruth got Debbie and Polly to help her in the missionary barrel.

"Let's go sort and put out the clothes," Debbie would say to Ruth when she wasn't satisfied with the clothes in her closet for school. But Ruth put out the clothes once a week, although daily she was picking up more boxes of clothes. It kept her busy and she guesses that a couple of thousand dollars a week went through the missionary closet.

Once a week Debbie and the girls went over to the basement of the seminary administration building to pull everything out of the large cedar closet that the original owners had installed (the seminary had purchased a 100-acre estate). Ruth laid out the clothes throughout the student commons. Most everything she laid out each week was quickly taken. The rules that Ruth made for the girls, she applied to herself.

> Take what you can use,
>
> Use what you can take.

Anyone who knows my wife, knows her elegance shines through, no matter what she wears. And that no matter what the cost of the clothes she wears, her character and dignity always is greater. It is definitely the case that she makes her clothes, and not the reverse, that her clothes make her. As Ruth visited the different women on the exclusive north shore of Chicago to pick up "hand-me-downs," for the missionary closet, she met ladies who were impressed with my wife. They listened to why Ruth helped young seminarian wives get through school. As a result, women told their friends and the missionary closet flourished under Ruth's leadership, perhaps bigger than it had ever been in the past. Ruth didn't just receive clothes as a "welfare" gift for someone who was poor. She made the donors realize they were "investing" their clothes in the ministry of quality young people who would lead the church into the future.

PRINCIPLES TO TAKE AWAY

1. The principle of the unmuzzled ox. The Word of God teaches not "to muzzle the ox that treadeth out the corn." This means that when you plow a field, the animal that pulls the plough should also be allowed to eat some of the corn in the row. In the same way, Ruth kept some of the clothes for herself and our children. They were able to dress better than we were able to afford on my salary.

2. The principle that humility opens the door to elegance. Ruth took a job that I didn't want her to have, because I didn't think it was dignified. But through the doorway of humility, she was able to serve the students, and ultimately dress better than we would have been able to afford if she had not said, "yes."

3. The "best" principle. I wanted to be the best, do the best, and accomplish the best for God in all that I did. And through a job to serve other people my wife, and children were able to dress the best, so that our total life would fulfill our desire of what we wanted to be for God.

CHAPTER SIXTEEN

THE MOVIES: NOT GOING NO LONGER

"Why can't we go to the movies?" Debbie brought up the question after dinner around the table.

Debbie was always the spokesperson for Sam and Polly. Whenever they wanted to step across a forbidden line, it was always Debbie who led Sam and Polly across. Even when asking for acceptable things, Debbie was the questioner. "Can we have ice cream?" Debbie asked for Sam and Polly. Debbie was the lawyer, questioning the decisions that we made. So, Debbie came and said,

"The other kids are going to the movies," and she added, "their parents are missionaries." She waited a moment to add, "Can we go?"

My family had been playing with the children from the Petker family; they were missionaries. In Debbie's mind missionaries were more spiritual than other people. They were more spiritual than us. I was just a teacher at a theological seminary, but missionaries went to the jungles where there were snakes and tigers. They preached the gospel to the heathen.

"If missionaries let their kids go to the movies," Debbie reasoned, "why can't we go with them?"

Going to the movies was a crucial issue of separation for my family. It was an issue we all had to face. Ruth had never been to a movie her entire life. She was reared by a fundamentalist father and mother who were against attending the Hollywood theater. I quit going to movies the day I was converted. At Columbia Bible College, Ruth and I were taught that movies were wrong. Our kids had not been to the movies.

We had taught our kids that movies were wrong. I say, "taught" because we used our family discussions around the table after meals to discuss the issues of life. When the kids got older, our discussions centered on what the kids would and could not do. While most families put a lot of emphasis on the family altar or family devotions, most of our training was done after the meal around the table where we discussed Christian issues and applied them to our family.

"You can't go to movies," I had told the kids, "because movies contain swear words... and violence, ...and are anti-Christian." I tried to explain to the kids how movies would damage their Christian lives, i.e. movies would make them sin.

"But we see movies on television..." Debbie would argue.

I tried to explain to Debbie that movies on television were censored, meaning sexual stuff was cut out and the cuss words were bleeped out.

I even explained to the kids that I preached at a lot of churches that had convictions against attending movies, and if we went to the movies, I couldn't go back to preach at those churches. The churches where I preached had high expectations for leadership, and I explained to my kids that their churches expected the entire family to live by those rules.

This time Debbie came to me with a new argument. "The missionary kids are going..." then Debbie went on to announce, "it's a Walt Disney movie that doesn't have any sex or cuss words." The movie in question was, *Mine, Yours, and Ours*. It was a cute Doris Day movie that basically had family values, I don't think it was a Walt Disney production. So, I said to Debbie,

"We will discuss it after dinner."

After we ate that evening, we brought up the issue of movies.

The Movies: Not Going No Longer

Again, I explained to the kids that we didn't go to movies because of (1) sex, (2) cursing, and (3) violence. I thought about it all day. I wanted to do the right thing and make the right decision. That night after dinner I said to them, "the whole attitude in Christianity is changing."

"Most Christians are now going to the movies," that doesn't make it right, but we live in this kind of world. Many of the churches that had been against movies, now were silent.

"No one in our family will go until we all vote that it is the right thing to do," was my conclusion. I didn't want to make the decision alone, although I had no trouble with decision-making. I wanted to give the family permission to discuss it and to vote on it. The kids were in their early teens, and soon they would be making their own decisions about movies and other areas of separation. So, I wanted them to discuss the issue within the family and decide within the family. If I made the decision, they would not feel accountable for going or not going. But if we made the decision together, everyone would feel accountable.

I wondered how Ruth would vote, but she was agreeable, so was Debbie and Polly. It was Sam who voted against movies, and for a couple of days, we continued discussing the movie issue. After a few days Sam said,

"I'm ready to go."

With Sam's agreement, we had a unanimous vote, so the kids could go to the movies. But I added,

"Mom and Dad will not go, because people look up to our leadership," I explained. "Since we don't have to go," I reasoned, "why should we attend movies?"

Debbie, Sam and Polly went to the movies to see *Mine, Yours, and Ours.* The missionary kids had made a practice of going to the movies, so it was no big deal to them.

When my kids came home that evening, I was concerned about their experience. I wanted to know what they saw, what they felt, what they experienced. To me this was one of those defining moments in life. I felt the whole course of human history turned on movie attendance. I asked if she liked the movie,

"It's fine..."

"That's all?"

"That's all."

"It was fine."

"Anything else?"

"No."

To my surprise I found out, it was no big deal to the kids. It was not a defining moment to them. So, this "passage" in life happened without fanfare. We let the kids go to see *Mine, Yours, and Ours*, but I knew they would want to go to another movie. The problem was, the Petker children left on missionary furlough. "Who would take our kids to the movies?" So, I put the movie issue out of my mind until I was confronted with *The Sound of Music*.

"We want to see *The Sound of Music*," Debbie said.

Here was another movie that had no sex, no violence, and no cuss words. The kids wanted to see it, but it was Debbie who scaled the mountain to ask the questions. After dinner she asked, "Can we go to see *The Sound of Music?*"

"Who's going to take you?"

"You and mom."

"Us?"

"Yes."

It was one thing for my children to attend the movies with the

Petker children who were missionary kids; after all, missionary kids are "spiritual." But our children did not have anyone to go with, and they wanted us to go to a movie. Debbie reminded us,

"*The Sound of Music* is groovy, no sex, no cursing, and no violence."

Then Ruth reminded us the story behind the movie was true, having the values we wanted to communicate to our children. *The Sound of Music* was about family, about children who overcame adversity, and how true love conquered the tyranny of Nazism. Ruth told how the VonTrapp family came to a town in Vermont where her mother lived as a child. Ruth knew the whole story because her mother knew the story behind the people in the film.

"I don't see why you can't go..." Debbie said.

With her childish logic, she told the truth. There was no reason why Ruth and I shouldn't take the kids as a family to see *The Sound of Music*.

I had been to the movies as a boy. The children had seen *Mine, Yours, and Ours*, but this was Ruth's first movie to see in a theater. This was the first time that she had ever been in a commercial theater in her life.

"Wadya think," I asked her.

"No big deal," she responded.

"No big deal."

"Then let's go."

We went to see *The Sound of Music*. It was an enjoyable experience and I felt it was something that was the right thing to do.

A couple of months later *Gone With the Wind* was re-introduced into the movies. Originally, *Gone With the Wind* had been released commercially almost twenty years earlier. The movie was an event, and we decided as a family to see *Gone With the Wind*. As a matter of fact, we had to travel forty miles to find a theater where it was being shown.

On the way to the movie, I set up some guidelines. I knew there was one curse word in the movie. Right at the very end of *Gone With the Wind* was the "D____" word. So, I explained to the children, we were seeing a movie that had one bad word.

I held up one finger to justify our actions, "But it has ONLY one bad word."

Almost mocking me the kids held up one finger and said,

"It has ONLY one bad word."

I was anxious to see *Gone With the Wind* because it told the story of Georgia during the post-Civil War days, tracing the history of the South to the beginning of the 1900s. I had grown up in Georgia and South Carolina. A lot of the experiences in *Gone With the Wind* were similar to my boyhood experiences. I wanted my children to understand the experiences I had as a child.

When buying the tickets, I asked the clerk if the one curse word had been bleeped out or if it still was in the soundtrack. He held up one finger saying,

"It has ONLY one curse word."

We sat through the first section of *Gone With the Wind*, and during the halftime break, we got popcorn, and cold drinks. Then we came in for the second half. Right at the very end of the film, Clark Gable playing the role of Rhett Butler, got to that memorable scene where he said, "Frankly my dear, I don't give a D___." Looking down the row I saw all of my children hold up one finger and say simultaneously,

"ONLY one curse word."

They didn't say the word. In the car on the way home they continued to mock, holding up one finger and repeating, "ONLY one curse word."

We laughed.

PRINCIPLES TO TAKE AWAY

1. <u>The principle of understanding</u>. Many parents just tell their children "No!" without giving them reasons why they can't do what they asked. Obviously, when children are small, they can be forced to obey, without being given a reason for their obedience. However, as they grow older, they become rebellious when they don't understand reasons why rules are made. That is, they become rebellious if they have high intelligence or a creative nature, which is what you want in your children. On the other hand, some children are forced to obey, but their will is squashed, so much so, that they introvert their personality. They become passive, and passive children do not aggressively reach their potential.

2. <u>The principle of inquisitiveness</u>. It is only natural for children to ask, "why?" When children ask for a reason behind a rule, they are not rebellious, they are not defying your authority, they are simply being children. One of the great drives God put into children is a drive to learn what they don't know. And God's way to learn is the question HE put within their head, "why?"

3. <u>The principle of listening</u>. Listening is one of the most difficult of all principles for parents to learn. Because parents are the authority in the home, many times they do not listen to their children. Since parents think they have taught children all that their child knows, they can't learn anything from their children. Parents get to the place where they do not listen to their children because they think their children do not know as much as them. Parents are right, children do not know as much as parents, but parents do not know what their children think. So, parents need to listen. Our children are made in the image of God, they are intellect, emotion and will. They have self-direction and self-perception. Children are learning from parents, and learning from many other people. When the parents are doing a good job, then their children are learning much more than what their parents are teaching them. As a result,

there comes a time when children know something their parents don't know and can contribute to their parents. When Debbie asked the question, "Why can't we go to the movies," she made me think through the reasons why I was making rules. I learned something from her.

4. <u>The principle of reasonable shift</u>. Most Christians are taught to be firm in their beliefs, and never compromise with sin. Christians are taught to never give up their convictions. As a result, they resist any change in their attitude toward sin, or toward their perception of sin. It was very difficult for me to change my attitude toward attending movies. When I became saved, I promised God that I would give up movies or any other thing that I felt was sin. I kept that promise for may years, until I attended *The Sound of Music* with my family. When I attended, I felt I was doing something with my family that promoted family values.

5. <u>The principle of slight attachment</u>. When I went to see *The Sound of Music* with my children, I had not been to the movies for approximately seventeen years. That is a long time, and I don't feel that I had not missed much, because attending movies was not my primary aim in life. Approximately four years after we attended *The Sound of Music*, I left Trinity Evangelical Divinity School and helped Jerry Falwell begin Liberty University (called Lynchburg Baptist College in its original days). Liberty University was a fundamentalist school, and from the beginning had a "no movie" rule, so it was very easy for me to keep the "no movie" rule. Obviously, I do not feel that my spirituality is tied to staying away from movies, nor do I think that I will lose my spirituality by attending movies, i.e. that is most "G" movies. So, when my wife and I associated with Liberty University, it was no big deal for us to quit going to movies. By that time, our children were old enough to make their own decisions about attending movies.

CHAPTER SEVENTEEN

I SPY: DEVELOPING THE POWER OF OBSERVATION

The family was sitting at the dining room table on Central Avenue in Deerfield, Illinois. Ruth was finishing up her meal, all the rest of us had eaten dinner quickly. Because she served the food and waited on the kids, she was always the last one to finish eating. So, I wouldn't let the kids leave the table before Ruth had finished eating. One evening I announced,

"I SPY...," then I waited a minute and said, "I SPY red."

Because we had just moved into Central Avenue, the decorations were not up. The dining room walls were bare, and there was a simple white tablecloth on the table. The table had been set with the necessary utensils, plus the condiments that were for the hamburgers.

"Let's play a game," I said to the kids. I told them, "The name of this game is 'I SPY'..." I explained that they had to guess what I saw.

"I SPY red."

"It's the ketchup bottle," yelled Debbie.

"No."

"I don't see anything else that is red," Debbie said.

"Look a little closer..." Then I explained that red might be on a package or in the design of a plate. Red could be the red letters on an advertising label.

"The red flower in the plate," Sam jumped into the conversation.

"No."

"It's the Nabisco seal," Debbie answered.

"Yes!"

Then it was Debbie's turn. That first time we played I SPY, she took a long time looking around and finally said, "I SPY white."

"Sugar," yelled Sam.

"No."

"White on the saltines box," Ruth replied.

"No."

"Salt ...," Polly got up on her knees and pointed to the saltshaker. We could barely see a little salt in the bottom of the glass container. "Salt is white," Polly emphasized the reason for her answer.

"Yes."

This game proceeded for the next five to ten minutes. First Debbie won, then Polly, and then Sam. I SPY went from green leaves in the center piece to silver forks, to brown hamburgers, and to green broccoli.

I felt that the game "I SPY" would be an excellent way to enhance the kids' powers of observation. It would teach them to be quick, and to be observant, and to be inventive. The next night we were sitting at the table and when everyone finished their meal I said,

I Spy: Developing the Power of Observation

"I SPY seven."

Debbie picked up the Worcestershire sauce bottle and examined it carefully. When she saw a seven, she pointed to it and asked, "Is it the seven on the Worcestershire sauce bottle?"

"No."

Both Polly and Sam reached over and picked up articles on the table and examined them for numbers. They began asking me about various numbers and finally Sam asked, "Is it 7 ounces of crackers?" He was holding the saltines in his hand pointing to the small seven in the corner. Actually, the seven was so small that most people would miss it unless they studied the package carefully.

"Yes."

When I said, "I spy seven" that lifted I SPY to a higher level of looking for small numbers on boxes, bottles, or any other packages on the table. Looking for numbers continued for several nights, then I decided to take I SPY to an even higher level. The next night after the meal, I looked around the table and announced, "I SPY five."

Immediately Debbie, Sam and Polly picked up packages to examine them for a number five. Every time they found a five, they asked if it were the object I spied.

"No."

Finally, Debbie in frustration said to me, "There's not another five on the table. How can you spy a five?"

"You've got to count five," I explained. "I spy five of the same things." "Five plates," answered Sam.

"No."

"Five glasses," answered Polly. "No."

The kids began counting everything at a place setting, thinking one of them had to be the answer because there were five people in the family. They automatically thought that it would be something like five forks. "Look at the forks very carefully," I told the kids. "Remember I said to you there are five of these things." "Five prongs," Debbie piped up first.

"Yes."

During the next few nights we played the game, "I SPY Green", or "I SPY Five", or "I SPY a Total of Five things." Each night the competition was getting more intense, while we upped the ante. Each night we had to make the object of spying a little more difficult to find. But that was great because the kids were becoming more inventive. I was accomplishing my goal. The next night when we sat down, as we waited to play I SPY, I announced to the kids,

"I SPY twenty-six..."

"That's a tough one," Ruth griped. They began to look for the number twenty-six on packages or containers but couldn't find it. Then they began to count different things, but each time they didn't have the right answer. Finally, Ruth figured it out. She said,

"I SPY twenty-six sides on the vase." There was a cut glass vase on the table, that was cut in odd sizes. During the evening meal I had counted the sides and there were twenty-six. Since that was an unusual number, I counted two or three more times and each time it came out to be twenty-six.

The stakes got higher and higher. One night, Ruth stumped us all with,

"I SPY 136."

"What?" I barked. "There's no such thing as something with 136 things." "Yes, there is... I counted them."

Finally, we all gave up. No one could find the 136 things or 136 printed numbers. One by one we all gave up. Then Ruth picked up the meat fork with 3 prongs and the salad fork with six prongs. We had not noticed, she had set the table with a salad fork, and a dessert fork and a regular fork. When we counted all the prongs on the table, there were 136 prongs.

The highest level was the combination of added numbers. One night I announced, "I SPY 248."

That was a toughie, but Ruth figured it out. It was the total addition of the numbers of a registered copyright on a commercial packet. That was about as tough as I SPY went in the family. Since we had escalated the game to an intolerable height, we stopped playing I SPY for the total addition of printed numbers. It was too hard. Then, it was to boring to go back to the bland I SPY, so we all lost interest.

Even though we stopped playing I SPY, I felt the game had a positive contribution to my children and they grew in their mental quickness. I SPY was a productive definable moment in their growth through the "wonder years."

PRINCIPLES TO TAKE AWAY

1. The principle that we learn the lessons to which we give attention. To make my children more observant of details, I thought that a game of I SPY would motivate them be aware of the details of life about them. When they became aware of facts and data, they could draw better conclusions in life.

2. The principle of fun learning. I felt that when kids have a fun time learning, they will learn more, learn better, and keep it longer. I also know they forget what they hated to learn. Therefore, I used the game I SPY to motivate them to learn more about the world around them, and to enjoy the journey.

3. The principle that competition brings out the best in all of us. When one of the family members correctly identified the I SPY

object, they had a chance to stump the rest of the family. Hence everyone in the family wanted to win, because they wanted to show their best. So when my children tried a little harder to guess an answer, they paid more attention to the facts of the world about them then they would in ordinary circumstances care.

There was also another fact about I SPY competition, no one was a loser. When a family member did not get the answer, they were not marked down for failing; nor did they lose. Only those who won were rewarded with being the leader for the next I SPY round. It was a game where we all eventually won and winning brings out the best in all of us.

4. <u>The principle of family togetherness</u>. It was important that our young family do things together, and the game I SPY brought us together. Sometimes our games lasted 30 minutes after the meal, that meant the kids were not quick to run off to watch T.V. or be with their buddies. We learned to enjoy one another, respect one another and play with one another.

CHAPTER EIGHTEEN

CHRISTMAS TREE ORNAMENTS: BUILDING FUTURE EXPECTATIONS

When we moved to Greater Chicago, Illinois, in 1965, I had been making $3,600 a year as a Bible college president. Many times, the donations at Winnipeg Bible College were not sufficient to pay salaries, so I had not always drawn my marginal salary of $300 a month.

We were poor, but we didn't act like it... we couldn't afford Christmas but had wonderful gifts... the Towns family was inventive. Christmas was always special, and we had more enjoyment of our Christmas without money than most families had with a lot of money. The particular year of 1965, I had made out a budget of the money available to spend on everyone for Christmas. Ruth and I only budgeted $5.00 a piece for ourselves. This $5.00 couldn't be spent on necessities, this was "mad" money we felt we could "blow" on non-essentials.

"Hey gang," I told the kids. "I've got a great idea for your mother's Christmas present."

"What," the kids chimed in.

"She wants a drip coffee maker..." I knew the kids would not be excited about buying her just a coffee pot, so I tried to build up some excitement in their minds.

"S-N-I-F-F," I made the sniffing sound. "She'll wake up every morning sniffing coffee."

"Oh Dad," Debbie was not enthusiastic.

"Mother will love this coffee pot because it makes the greatest smell of coffee... greater than any other coffee maker in the world ..." I tried to overcome their reluctance.

I explained how I got up early in the morning to make coffee in the percolator, the old one that was given to us as a wedding present twelve years earlier. But it was wearing out. The old coffee maker brewed perked coffee. Ruth wanted drip coffee because they had one at her office where she was a secretary.

"Your mother wants a drip coffee maker more than anything else in life," I exaggerated to the kids, knowing that Ruth would much rather have her own house, her own car, and her own new fur coat. I knew a drip coffee maker was far down Ruth's want list, but it was something we could afford. A drip coffee maker fell within the five dollars Christmas gift limit, so I decided,

"Your mother wants a drip coffee maker more than anything else in life."

"Let's get it," the kids agreed.

I got home at three o'clock to meet the kids when they came home from school, Ruth did not get off until five o'clock pm. It was a brisk winter day when the kids got home. It was only two blocks down to the Kress Five-n-Dime store. They had the coffee maker we wanted for only $3.80.

"That's within the five-dollar limit."

"Let's buy a pound of coffee," Sam said.

"Yeah," the girls said.

So, we bought the coffee maker and dropped by A&P grocery store to get a pound of fresh ground drip coffee... 8 o'clock coffee.

Those who remember the early drip coffee maker, remember it came in many pieces. The aluminum lid came with glass bubble on top, and the bubble popped out of the lid, making two pieces. Then there was a basket strainer, a lid and the stand making three pieces. Then the pot itself had the bottom part, the middle part, and the top part, making three pieces.

"Let's wrap it in eight boxes," I said to the kids. "And let's camouflage it so she won't know."

"Yeah," Debbie said.

The little glass bubble on top was about the size of a marble. We wrapped in a large dress box to make her think that she was getting something big... maybe a dress.

"Let's put a brick in the package with the basket," Sam said to make it heavier.

"Yeah."

We ended up with eight packages of various sizes. Then there was the one package of about a pound of 8 o'clock coffee making nine packages. It was a pound of coffee, so that package weighed about a pound.

On Christmas morning, there were nine different gifts, wrapped in nine different ways, all for Ruth. The kids wanted her to open first, even before they got to their presents. Their excitement over a simple drip coffee maker had captured their imagination.

"Open this one first," Polly squealed. It was the large dress box; Ruth couldn't find the glass bubble in all of the wrappings. Finally, she held it up,

"What's this?"

Laughter erupted among the children.

"Guess!"

After she opened the second package, Ruth guessed it was the drip coffee pot she had asked for.

Christmas has always had special traditions in the Towns family. While some religious traditions perpetuate dead ideas, other traditions are good; because they remind us of enduring truth. The Santa Claus poster is one of those traditions.

Each year on December the first, Ruth made a large red Santa and hung it over the wooden front door, always protected behind the storm door. Since we usually had a glass storm door, people coming up our walk could see our large friendly red Santa at our door. Actually, it was not a picture of Santa at all. Ruth covered the whole door with red wrapping paper. Then she cut out a white nose, white mouth, white eyes, and a white cap and posted them where the head should be. There were white buttons down the belly, and a black belt made the belly big and jolly. A couple of black boots were pasted on, and Santa became our welcome card to visitors during the Christmas season.

Ruth always put up the red Santa while I put up the Christmas tree. We always did it on the first of December. Why? Because we always did it on December the first. No reason, it was just our tradition.

Another tradition was the way we opened our presents on Christmas morning. Because I had seen individuals tearing into their presents and no one watching or enjoying what the others in the family got. I felt a lot of fun was lost. The parents were usually helplessly looking from one child to the other to try to take it all in. So, I decided that we would open our presents one at a time. Debbie always opened a present first, Sam second, and Polly last.

"You go first Debbie," I instructed, and we all watched what she got. If it was clothing, we waited while she put it on. If it was a toy we waited while she tried it out. Sometimes we even waited because, "some assembly was required."

"You next Sam," he followed the same procedure.

"Polly it's your turn."

Then it was Ruth's turn and finally I came last. We followed this sequence until all of the presents were opened. While most families rip all the presents open in ten or fifteen minutes, it usually took us two or more hours to open gifts; but we enjoyed one another's presence more.

We usually had a turkey for Christmas dinner. When I was a college president, I went to a board member who was passing turkeys out to his employees and asked that he purchase a turkey for all of my faculty. Filling the trunk of my car with frozen turkeys, I drove around on Christmas Eve delivering one to every faculty member. The college where I was president was not able to give a Christmas bonus or gift. But the gift of a turkey was appreciated.

As soon as Christmas dinner was over, Ruth and I have always taken down the tree. For us, when Christmas is over, it's over. We've enjoyed it for 25 days, let's move on. As soon as dinner was over, the dishes were washed and the food was put away, Ruth announced, "Christmas is over," she said with a sigh, "let's take down the tree."

The ornaments came down and were placed back in the same box for next year. I hauled the tree outside, threw it by the curb for the garbage man, and Christmas was over.

There was an overriding reason to finish Christmas. Ruth's birthday was the day after Christmas. She was born on December 26, 1932. She warned us about writing "Happy Birthday" on a Christmas card, and she told the kids to never wrap her birthday gift in Christmas paper. So, on December 25, we put Christmas behind and move on to celebrate Ruth's birthday.

Perhaps one of the most meaningful Christmas traditions, is the Christmas tree ornament tradition. I don't know exactly how it got started, but it has lasted for forty years. When Debbie was first born, we bought a Christmas tree ornament, and wrote her name on it, and dated the ornament. We hung it on the tree and announced, "When she gets married, she can hang that ornament on her tree." Even when we were first married, Ruth and I were aware of the power of traditions.

A year later we had two children, Sam came along thirteen months after Debbie. So we bought two Christmas ornaments, wrote Debbie Jean, 1956 on one, and Stephen Richard (Sam), 1956 on the other.

We continued the tradition the next year, keeping the family ornaments in a special box, obviously the number of ornaments got larger each year.

In 1958, Polly came along and we bought three ornaments that year, one for Debbie, one for Sam and one for Polly.

Today our Christmas tree does not have the family ornaments. When Debbie got married, she took hers with her. Polly was the next to get married and she took hers with her. So, did Sam.

PRINCIPLES TO TAKE AWAY

1. The principle that it doesn't take money to make kids happy. When my kids talk about their happiest Christmas ever, they always remember the Christmas where we bought a "lot" of gifts for Ruth (the drip coffee pot). But it was not just Ruth, we also wrapped a lot of presents for me, for Grandmother Towns, and for Uncle Richard. There were so many small presents under the tree, that it seemed to take all morning to unwrap the gifts. We were poor, but the kids remember it as one of the happiest Christmases ever. There were no big gifts that year. Remember, happiness is found on the journey, more than the destination.

2. The principle of the future looking backwards. I feel that tradition is something we look forward to, such as Santa Claus on the front porch or an ornament for each child each year. And in looking forward to the future, we automatically look back to how it originated in the past; and in looking forward and backwards, we remember its meaning.

3. The "moving on" principle. We look forward to Christmas for 25 days, beginning to decorate our house on December 1st. But after we opened the presents and ate the turkey, we were ready to move on. We took down our Christmas tree on Christmas Day and dumped it on the curb with the used Christmas wrappings. We were ready to move on to a new year.

4. The "planned tradition" principle. We purposely planned to make our children traditionalist, by telling them each year about their past Christmas tree ornaments. Each year they knew that one gift would be a new Christmas tree ornament to hang on the tree. Unashamedly, Ruth and I were firmly making our kids traditionalist.

CHAPTER NINETEEN

FIRST CARS: TAKING RESPONSIBILITY

The family was sitting at the breakfast table in Lynchburg, Virginia. Ruth and I were sorting out the day's activities. I had a full day at the college; Ruth taught one course in the middle of the day. Besides that, we had to drive the kids to school, then there was cheerleading practice, and someone had to go back late at night to pick up Sam.

Debbie was 17, Sam was 16, and Polly was 14. They all attended Lynchburg Christian Academy which didn't have bus service. Getting the kids around was a daily problem. We only had one car. As we finished breakfast, Sam said,

"If you bought me a car," Sam watched my eyes for a response, then said, "you wouldn't have to drive us to school each day."

"Oh," was all I said.

"I could drive us to school each day," Sam was referring to his sisters.

"Yeah," Debbie said, "Dr. Guillermin bought his daughter a car; she drives her sister to school each day."

Debbie was describing the principal of the Christian school. Dr. Guillermin had bought his daughter a car, and each day the two girls drove to school. Dr. Guillermin's daughters were approximately one year older than my children. So, I was expected to follow the example. Because the Guillermin girls were responsible, I thought it was appropriate for them to have a car. But I knew some children in the Christian school were irresponsible. Just because their parents were saved, and their children, it didn't mean they had character.

"What about Suzie," I threw the question out to the kids, "Her parents bought her a brand-new car, she wrecked it within a year."

Then I began to think about all the headache I'd have if my kids owned a car. I thought "WOULD THEY TAKE RESPONSIBILITY OF THE CAR ... TO CHANGE THE OIL ... TO DRIVE SAFELY ... TO MAKE SURE THAT REPAIRS WERE MADE?" I had enough headaches looking after my car, I didn't want more headaches. So, I added,

"And don't forget about Jimmie," I wanted to make a point. "He had three different fender-benders this year," I added. "Then there is a problem of cruising ... I don't want you cruising in my car."

"But Dad," Sam said, "we've always been responsible; we've been more responsible than other kids."

Sam was right. Our kids were always more responsible than other kids. They had learned well the value of money and personal property.

"Let me give it some thought for the next couple of days," I told Sam. "I promise you we will talk about it again."

Over the next two or three days, I thought about it. There was no doubt we needed another car. Sam was old enough to drive and own a car. So, what kind of car was I going to get. I was not able to afford a brand-new car; I didn't buy a new car for myself. I usually bought the one-year old model, to bypass the extreme depreciation the first year. On the other hand, I didn't want to buy them a junker; it would be untrustworthy.

I prayed for guidance. I asked God for wisdom to make a good decision. Several days later I was ready to discuss the topic again.

"I have a proposal for you about a car," I announced at the dinner table.

"What is it ...," all three kids seemed to ask in unison.

"I think I ought to help each of you buy a car," I said to the kids, "but I don't think I ought to pay the whole price." I explained that I would apply the same principle to all three kids.

Sam furrowed his forehead like he was thinking through what I proposed. He wanted to ask some questions but didn't. Sam knew he needed some financial help, so he just listened.

"What does that mean?" Debbie was always the one to ask.

"I think I ought to pay half of the price of a car," I explained. "If you buy a cheap car, it won't cost me much. But if you buy an expensive car, I'll put as much money in your car as you will." I waited for them to think about the offer then said, "It'll be your car ... your title deed . . . your responsibility . . . and I'll pay half."

This was a perfect answer to our problem. The car would belong to them, be registered in their name, and insurance would be taken out in their name. I promised to pay half of the insurance per year, knowing insurance for young people was much higher than for adults.

"How much money do you have saved," I turned to Sam, knowing he would be the first to purchase a car. He was the saver in the family. He had a secret account at the bank, and he still had some mutual funds I purchased for him. In addition, Sam had two or three secret hiding places in his room where he "squirreled" away coins and paper money.

"I'll have to go count it," Sam got up, left the table and went to count his shekels.

When Sam looked back on the conversation about getting a car, he confessed to only wanting permission to buy a car, not to get money from his dad. He was thinking "cheap." I was thinking "reliable." But buying a car for your son is one of the privileges of being a father. In one sense I wanted to pay the whole price. But on the other hand, I wanted Sam to take "ownership"; hence, to take "accountability," he had to literally "buy" into the transaction.

When he returned to the table he announced, "I have over six hundred dollars."

"Wow," I spoke without thinking. "You've got that much."

"I have at least six hundred dollars to spend on a car..." he smiled a sheepish grin.

"That means you have more, but you don't want to spend it," I again was surprised.

"Right."

"Let's go car shopping after school tomorrow."

"Right."

Only a father understands what it means to take his son to buy his first car. A car is not just steel, glass, tires and carburetors under the hood. A car means independence, power, and it raises a boy's self-perception among his buddies. When a boy in high school owns a car, his life is elevated to a new level. He thinks different about himself; he becomes different.

We toured five or six used-car lots that first afternoon looking at Fords, Chevrolets, and Toyotas.

"No old Chrysler products," I said. "We don't want a taxi or police car."

First Cars: Taking Responsibility

"I don't want an old boat," Sam announced. "I want something that is <u>zippy</u>... something that is <u>sporty</u>... something that is cool."

I understood cool; I had been a kid once.

Sam must have driven a dozen cars during the afternoon, always heading straight for the Lynchburg Expressway where he put the accelerator to the floor and moved out... to the max. Then he headed for a rough, rocky dirt road, where he could hit the brakes and spray on the rocks.

"I don't want a four door," Sam observed, "old people drive four door cars."

So, it had to be a two door, sporty... zippy... cool... wheels.

Finally, we went across the James River from Lynchburg, Virginia, into Madison Heights, finding "John P. Hughes Used Cars."

Sam saw a 1968 gold Chevy Nova... a two-door car that was zippy... sporty... cool... exactly what he was looking for.

Like Anthony seeing Cleopatra, or Romeo seeing Juliet... It was love at first sight. He wanted it before he drove it.

But there was a large $1299 price tag written in white shoe polish on the front window. The Nova was the car that Sam wanted, but it was $100 above his limit. Sam was going to give $600 and I was going to give $600. We were shopping for an $1200 used car.

The traffic was whizzing past us on US Route 29 in Madison Heights, but Sam and I didn't hear anything. I pointed to the $1299 price on the front of the car and said,

"Are you willing to go an extra $50," I directed my question to Sam. "I'll add $50. That'll do it."

Sam shook his head "no."

"I've got to have money for insurance, gas," he knew exactly how much money he had. "I can't go beyond $600."

As I stood there, I knew it was a good buy. Sam didn't want to lose the car. I could have easily given the extra $100, but I wanted Sam to feel ownership. I didn't know what to do.

For the next minute, Sam and I talked about the difference between $1200 and $1299 and making up the difference. We were not trying to negotiate prices with John Hughes the owner. We were just talking among ourselves.

"I just can't go the extra," Sam's words reflected his disappointment, "let's go back and look at the Mustang."

"Don't do that," John Hughes interrupted our conversation. "If you'll give me $1200 today, you can drive it home."

Sam reached into his pocket and pulled out a wad of twenty-dollar bills and began counting them one by one into John Hughes open hand. The identity of John Hughes has endured in Lynchburg, and today he advertised his as the oldest car sales in Lynchburg. I wrote my check for $600 and added the price for tax, title and registration. John Hughes took a screwdriver and bolted the temporary cardboard license on the zippy... sporty... cool... Nova. Then I had the greatest thrill in life, I stood there with John Hughes and together we watched Sam climb into that zippy... sporty... cool... Nova and drive off the parking lot heading south toward Lynchburg.

The decision was good for me, because Sam took responsibility for his car and never once did I have to worry about gas, repair or changing the oil. It was Sam's car; it was totally his car and I never once had a worry in the world.

At the time Sam was an evening janitor at Thomas Road Baptist Church. His job was primarily to mop the floors, strip the wax, and re-wax the floors. Of course, there were other jobs, but the floors were his primary duty. He made enough money as a janitor to keep his car running. As a matter of fact, Sam's kept his Nova in such top rate running conditions, that Lynchburg Christian Academy used it for their Driver Education Program. They couldn't afford their own. So, Sam negotiated with the office for gas and insurance money for the use of his car. Of course, Sam was in the class and knew how to drive; but he still had to take the class to graduate. So, Sam and his friends who could already drive used his car to pass the course.

Debbie was the next to purchase a car, and the same rule applied. She bought a 1969 Volkswagen that she named "chigger," because it was a red bug. It cost more than Sam's car; the price was $1795. Both Debbie and I came up with $850 to pay for her "chigger."

Debbie was a waitress, and a very good one. She was friendly, smiled and hustled the meals to the table. Her tips were good, and once she got her car, she never had an accident, and I never had to worry about repairs, upkeep. Never a worry in the world. Again, it was an excellent principle to follow.

Polly was the last to purchase a car. She got a job at Ponderosa Steakhouse and like her sister, she was friendly, smiled, and hustled the meals out quickly. As a result, she also got good tips. When it came time to pay for her car, the price was $2495. Again, following the principle we had laid down with Sam, Polly and I each came up with $1250. Polly's first car was a gold Volkswagen bug, only a year old. It was a "sunbug." Like her sister and brother before her, Polly took full responsibility for her car. There was never an accident, repair, or any concern to me.

PRINCIPLES TO TAKE AWAY

1. The principle of ownership. When you give children something that they don't ask for they usually don't take care of it. Sometimes the same thing happens when you give them something they ask for. Just because children ask for something doesn't mean they'll take care of it. But when children "buy into" what they want, they usually take higher responsibility for that possession.

2. <u>The principle of accountability</u>. How can we teach children to be accountable for their possessions? When they buy something they really want with their own money, they usually take pride of ownership, and quickly thereafter accountability follows. As much as parents want to give an automobile to children when they turn sixteen, or when they graduate from high school, or from college, not all children will take care of what is given them. Children will usually take care of what they have to work for.

3. <u>The principle of "passages."</u> There are certain times in life when our children pass from one stage to a whole new level of living. That happens when your son gets his first car. On that May afternoon my son passed from childhood into the adult world. As we stood at John Hughes Autos, my son and I experienced deep emotions, but in each the emotions were different. I was proud of my son for he was launching into the world of adult car ownership. Sam was proud of his car, and he was stepping into the world of independence. He had something that most of his buddies at school didn't have; he owned a car. He had now joined the ranks of adults, who purchased a major possession and was an owner of tangible property. Sam had to be responsible to the state by getting a driver's license and automobile registration, followed by a tag. He had to purchase automobile insurance, all making him a part of the adult world.

4. <u>The pride of ownership principle</u>. Even though I paid half the price of the car, I heard my adolescent son tell his friends that he bought his car. Now technically, that was the truth. He did buy his car, with some help from me. I don't ever remember him telling his buddies in high school that his father had helped in the purchase of the car. I did not need that affirmation, nor did I want it, nor did I ever rebuke him for what he said. When my son gave that toothy grin of his, I could tell that he was bragging when he said, "I bought my car." And his pride of ownership became my point of pride. It was Sam's car.

APPENDIX A

THE TOWNS' WAY: HOW TO TEACH CHARACTER TO CHILDREN

Of all the human things we do in life (notice I said human and not spiritual), our greatest task is teaching our children to live the right way for the right purpose.

This book will tell some stories of how we attempted to give our children a passion to live the right way for the right purpose. It does not attempt to glorify my wife and me, for we have made mistakes. This book will honestly tell how we did some wrong things, and we did some things the wrong way. This book does not attempt to glorify our children, for we know they were not angels. Sometimes they were mischievous.

Once I asked Sam why he didn't clean up his room when he was suppose to.

"Why?... Why?... Why?..." was a reflective question I asked Sam.

Sam smiled his innocent grin when I caught him doing something he shouldn't. He threw up both arms with a "gee whiz" attitude, and answered in the words of a singer in his youth, Jimmy Rogers,

I'm a child of clay,

Shaped and molded into what I am today.

This phrase from a popular song was my son's way of saying he made mistakes just like I did when I was a boy.

HOW TO TEACH CHARACTER

The Bible says, "Train up a child in the way he should go, and when he is old, he will not depart from it" (Proverbs 22:6, NKJV). Some parents have attempted to form character in their children and have been successful.   Other parents have failed. Over the years, I have found that just because parents were Christians, didn't automatically guarantee their children would live for Christ. Some Christians have failed with their children, while many other Christian parents have produced wonderful Christian children. Why have some children, raised in Christian homes, gone bad? While this is not a negative book to point out the things Christian parents do wrong, some will see their mistakes and make corrections.

Making children do the right thing doesn't always work. Some children never drank alcohol or smoke because their parents forced a strict behavior code on them. But as soon as the child left home, the child became a drunk. So, making children do the right is important in molding character, but it takes more than habit formation and conformity to build character into them.

Some instill a right ATTITUDE in their children, wanting them to turn out right. A little girl had a good attitude; she was a happy, positive little girl who laughed a lot. So, an unsuspecting boy thinks he is marrying a lovable doll, only to find out the smile was superficial. After they were married, she chronically complained about him because he couldn't live up to her standards. A good attitude will not insure biblical character.

Some think you influence your children by planting LOFTY DREAMS in their hearts. A child may have a vision of becoming a medical doctor, but their lifelong dream may never be realized if they are not taught daily discipline to get them through college and medical school. Just having a worthwhile dream will not ensure that a child will do the right thing in the right way, i.e., that the child will develop biblical character.

Some think their child will develop character because they ATTEND Sunday school where they are taught a Christian approach to life. The child's faith can become so real that they KNOW God exists and they ask Christ to forgive their sins. But when the child grows up, they mess up their marriage and can't hold a job. Their faith in God is never translated into daily practice. They fail in life. Just because a child has deep faith, doesn't mean he/she will necessarily develop character.

Some think when their children KNOW right from wrong, they will develop character. But children from good homes where mom and dad never even smoke cigarettes, end up smoking pot. Some kids know that drugs will hurt them, but they do drugs anyway. So, knowledge, whether by schooling or personal instruction by parents, will not necessarily guarantee that children will develop character.

Is there any guarantee that we can communicate biblical character to our children? Do we have any assurance that parents can make a difference? What my wife has called the Towns' Way is what we have learned about raising children. It's not any one of the above suggestions; it's all of them together. Making sure a child turns out properly is more than doing one thing or implementing one event. Character formation is a life long process and all these factors are necessary to influence the character of children.

Training a child involves HABIT FORMATION, but it takes more than continually doing right. Training a child involves controlling their ACTIONS, but it takes more than doing the right thing. Training a child involves ATTITUDE FORMATION, but it takes more than correct attitudes. Training a child involves DREAM FORMATION, but it takes more then giving them a vision of the future. Training a child involves FAITH FORMATION, but it takes more than faith and believing. Training a child involves knowledge, reasons and UNDERSTANDING. But it takes more than these—it takes all of these together. I have put these into a cycle that we can follow to develop character (see below).

Ruth and I did not begin with the Towns' Way; it grew out of our experience. At times we tried to build dreams in our children; at other times we worked on their habits. Now that we've finished the task, and we're working on grandchildren, we've come to see that training character in children involves many things, i.e. it involves all the things in this cycle.

Let me explain the cycle to you. Now obviously, just knowing the cycle will not guarantee you will raise your children properly. Also, it's impossible to do everything in sequence. I've suggested this cycle to give you an overall view of the process. This cycle is like looking at a ball game from a blimp, you get a big overall picture. Let me explain each step of the Towns' Way.

First, a parent must influence their child's thinking. A child must know what is right to understand their actions. Remember, in the story of "B-U-T-T: You Can't Say That," I had to teach the children that certain words are wrong. Now at age 40, Polly won't let her daughter say the "B___" word, because she believes it is inappropriate for children.

Christianity is a rational faith, and God wants us to understand Him and learn the principles that will please Him. While correct biblical knowledge will not save anyone, nor will correct knowledge give a child character, we cannot produce character if the children don't understand what they are doing. So, we begin with giving them reasons, knowledge and UNDERSTANDING.

Appendix A

Second, for the child to develop character, they must develop FAITH. Parents must help children believe in the principles taught them. Faith is when we "affirm what God has said in the Scriptures." Faith has been described as taking God at His Word. Therefore, our faith is a reaction to God. What I couldn't teach Debbie about faith, she learned in Mexico when she served the Lord mixing concrete, building pews and praying for a Gospel service. When Debbie felt about God the way I felt and responded to God the way I responded, she developed her faith as I had developed my faith.

The child's faith is never blind faith; they must act on what he has been taught because he knows it is right. While inculcating belief principles will not insure a child develops character, you cannot produce character if you do not include FAITH FORMATION in what you teach them.

Third, we develop character when we give the child VISION and DREAMS of what they can do or become in life. One way to develop character is to give them heroes who have the qualities we want our children to acquire. When children develop vision, they also are acquiring motivation. If they have a vision of living godly, they will probably acquire godliness. This book told stories of how I tried to make my children winners, by teaching them Monopoly. It also told how I tried to develop a desire in them to read great books by reading Classic Comics. We never had much money when my children were growing up, but I didn't want them to see themselves as poor, even when Debbie and Polly worked with Ruth in the Missionary Closet. I wanted them to be a "Towns ... who could do anything."

Producing VISION in your children is a step toward producing character, but a vision alone will not do it, there is another step.

The fourth step to build character is to develop GOOD ATTITUDES in your children. One mother said, "Make up your mind to have a good day before you make up your bed... and you will have a good day, whether it is or not." I didn't want my children to complain about no money, so I taught them to work to get McDonald's hamburgers. We all collated the book *Teaching Teens*, so we could all enjoy hamburgers. I tried to give them a good attitude about work. That's the point of the chapter about picking up firewood. The kids didn't want to do it, so I was challenged to find a way to make word fun. When we change our children's attitude toward manual work, we change their work habits.

While developing a good attitude is a step toward developing biblical character, making a child have a sweet attitude by itself will not develop character, it takes another step.

The fifth step to biblical character in children is making sure they do the right thing. This involves doing RIGHT ACTIONS. My mother use to tell me, "If you do it right, you will be right." That statement is correct, but it doesn't stand alone. Many children have gone to Sunday school and church all their childhood but quit when they got older. Good church attendance was only an outward action that did not result in inward character. I tried to force my children to enjoy the vacations we took. But they didn't want to get out of the car to see the sights. Character involves getting children to "do the right thing," but it must be "done in the right way." So, the story of the Photo Contest is not only getting children to do the right things, it was an attempt to get them to do it for the right purpose.

While forcing children to act right won't result in godly character in our children, we can't build character without correct actions. Then we must take another step.

The sixth step in molding character is HABIT FORMATION. When recruits go to boot camp, the sergeant controls every part of their life. The recruit is taught to say, "Yes Sir," dress properly, and think properly. The recruit is taught the military way of doing things. But just training a person in military habits, will not insure that is the way they will live. Recently, I met an unshaven former U.S. Marine with long hair, wearing dirty old clothes. He lived in a filthy trailer. Everything about him reeked of failure and self-indulgence. He forgot every military habit he acquired in the Marines.

Appendix A

We mold character when we mold habits, but habit formation by itself is never enough. To build character, parents must take a (1) total life approach from birth to when they leave home, and a (2) total experience approach, from thinking, to knowing, to dreaming, to doing.

Character is doing the right thing when no one is looking. The little boy is taught not to waste other people's time. He was never late to school, because his mother got him there on time. When can the mother know that her training was successful? She is successful when her boy develops a punctual lifestyle when not one is checking up on him. The boy developed the character trait of being on time, not because he knows it is beneficial, or even because it was his mother's habit; he's always on time, because that's the way he lives, that's him. He believes in being punctual, more than because of attitudes or actions; he is a punctual person because that's who he is.

You become a person of character,

when you live the biblical standards,

you've been taught to be.

Character does not come naturally to the growing child. The child is born with its fist clenched, reflecting a dominant selfish bent in life. The precious cuddly baby will grow up to be a mean spoiled brat, if he does not acquire the basic virtues of character, i.e. gratitude, thinking of others, etc. Character is not automatic in some and void in others. When you see a person who habitually does the right thing for the right purpose, someone trained that person.

Because a person has strong character traits in one area of their life, does not automatically guarantee they are well rounded, and will do all things right. I once knew a woman who was well-mannered, kind, gentle and punctual. There were so many beautiful qualities about her, but when she walked into her apartment, everything seemed helter-skelter. She never hung up her clothes, her bed was unmade, dishes were dirty, etc. But she was beautiful in most every other way.

The last point is the most important. It takes character in parents to produce character in children. It takes a right standard in parents to communicate a right standard to their children.

I'm thankful for all the good things my children do. They are hard-working people ... honest people ... they love their children and they are good to others. Their weaknesses are really my weaknesses. Because when they are weak in one area, it's because I didn't properly teach them "to do the right thing, in the right way."

THE TOWNS' WAY

When you guide your children's thinking according to the
Bible,

You influence the convictions they believe.

When you guide their beliefs by great vision,

You influence their attitudes.

When you guide the attitudes they value,

You influence their actions.

When you guide their everyday actions,

You influence their habits.

When you guide their habits,

You produce character.